A Question of Answers
Volume I

Primary Socialization, Language and Education
Edited by Basil Bernstein
University of London Institute of Education
Sociological Research Unit

A Question of Answers

Volume I

W. P. Robinson &
Susan J. Rackstraw

Department of Psychology
University of Southampton

ROUTLEDGE & KEGAN PAUL

London and Boston

First published 1972
by Routledge and Kegan Paul Ltd
Broadway House,
68–74 Carter Lane,
London, EC4V 5EL
and 9 Park Street, Boston, Mass. 02108 U.S.A.

Printed in Great Britain by
Clarke, Doble & Brendon Ltd
Plymouth

ISBN 0 7100 6986 3

Contents

Foreword

Dr Peter Robinson and Miss Susan Rackstraw were members of the Sociological Research Unit between 1964 and 1966. Dr Robinson was deputy head of the Unit, and Miss Rackstraw was involved in the analysis of the children's speech. This period 1964–6 was particularly hectic. The Unit was literally awash with data, for in the summer and early autumn of 1965 we had completed the interviews with the mothers in the middle-class area and we had collected the speech of their children. The language programme in the working-class area was entering its second year and we were beginning to think of how we were going to evaluate it. (See D. M. and G. A. Gahagan, *Talk Reform: An Exploratory Language Programme for Infant School Pupils*, Routledge & Kegan Paul, 1970.) The excitement of collecting the data had passed; the problem was its control. Tapes were played and re-played. The development of theoretically deprived taxonomic schemes became the focus of heated discussions, which appeared at times to have a cathartic rather than an intellectual function—a strange contrast to the bland impassiveness of the ritual form of the final report. Owing to the inadequate development of the theory at that period, the grammatical analysis of the children's speech was a particularly sensitive area. As a consequence, the linguists quite correctly felt that they were on a ship without a rudder. The sociologists, on the other hand, thought they had a rudder but could not find the ship. Looking back, it is easy to see that this was perhaps an inevitable stage in the life of research where there were few guiding procedures to deal with the questions which were being asked.

I write this to give some idea of the difficulties which faced Dr Robinson when he joined the research. At that particular time, we had not developed the linguistic analysis to anywhere near the sophistication of the social psychological analysis. Indeed, it took nearly four years to unite with any success these two levels. As a consequence, there is a marked indelicacy of Dr Robinson's and Miss Rackstraw's taxonomy at the levels of grammar and lexes. Such indelicacy limits our understanding of the relationships between semantic and linguistic choices. This is not written as a criticism, rather I regret that we were not able at that time to provide an adequate linguistic basis for Dr Robinson's and Miss Rackstraw's taxonomy. The pacing of research is such that later solutions rarely can be applied to earlier problems.

As with much of the Sociological Research Unit's work, these two volumes attempt to go beyond a specific research question in order to seek out a general framework for exploring a class of problems. The taxonomic scheme had its source in a particular problem, but it ended as a broad theoretical framework for interpreting question-answer exchanges. It is interesting to see how the scheme began in the first empirical paper, and its greater sophistication in the last empirical paper in Volume I. From this point of view it is unfortunate that it was not possible to include in this volume Dr Robinson's final paper in the empirical series, in which he shows the relationship between the answering styles of the mothers to the answering styles of their children. (This paper is included in *Class Codes and Control*, Volume II, edited by Basil Bernstein, Routledge & Kegan Paul, forthcoming.)

The reader will notice that the research papers are based upon samples which are matched for a range of variables. As a consequence the matching of mothers or children is achieved at the cost of the numbers in each sub-group. It is sometimes a little surprising to find, that given the range of controls and such small numbers in each sub-group, this combination does yield critically significant differences. It is quite clear, at least to me, that the potentiality of the authors' taxonomy could not be fully realized because of the constraints of the size of the sample and the relatively small size of the individual texts. I must take responsibility for these constraints. Dr Robinson's and Miss Rackstraw's project was one of a great number of projects which we were investigating. It might be said that the Unit attempted too much and as a result each individual project suffered. However, I believe we all saw the research as exploring areas rather than attempting definitive studies. Any one of the individual projects could itself have been the subject of a separate and wide-ranging enquiry.

I shall not comment on the findings as these are extensively discussed in the various chapters. It is, however, very interesting to learn from Chapter 7 that the working-class girls who were members of the language programme sample (see D. M. and G. A. Gahagan) produced answers which were more similar to the answering behaviour of the middle-class girls than the working-class girls who had not taken part in the programme. On the whole, no one will quarrel with the authors' conclusion that much of the variance is still hidden under the social class blanket; that is, although there are major differences between the children and mothers which relate to their respective social class position, we cannot tell from this study what *specific* features of social class position account for the differences. It is possible that we shall be in a better position to account for these differences when we have analysed the wide-ranging second interview of the mothers which, far more than the first interview, examined in some detail aspects of the family structure and forms of communication.

Despite the constraints, Dr Robinson and Miss Rackstraw have produced a pioneering study.

BASIL BERNSTEIN

Acknowledgments

We are very pleased to record our thanks to the organizations which financed the research reported: the Department of Education and Science, the Ford Foundation, and the Joseph Rowntree Memorial Trust. All members of Professor Bernstein's Sociological Research Unit at the Institute of Education, London, played some part in the work, but we would like to thank Miss Suzanne Biggs, W. Brandis and C. D. Creed particularly for their help with data collection and processing.

We are most grateful to Mrs M. Jackson and Miss F. M. Freeman for typing, checking and correcting the manuscript and proofs, and to Miss D. M. Marshallsay for a most carefully prepared index.

The Clarendon Press has kindly allowed us to include a slightly amended version of an article first published in *Sociology*, 1967, i, 'Variations in mothers' answers to children's questions as a function of social class', and the Editor of *Language and Speech* has given similar permission for an article first published in 1967, vol. 10, 'Social and psychological factors related to variability of answering behaviour in 5-year-old children'.

Chapter 1   Outline of research

1   What the problems are

Question: 'Why shouldn't you tell lies?'
Answer: 'Because it's naughty. Because then they tell lies. They um tell a er a he and then they um when they tell a lie they er when they er tell a lie the er the their mothers says, "All right then", but ha then their mothers don't think um it's a lie.'

It is a quaint custom to insert enigmatic quotations at the beginning of chapters, but they do provide a certain amount of fun when we try to work out the relationship, if any, between the quote and the contents of its associated chapter, and we may rarely experience a glow of undue pride when we recognize its origin. Ours is not from Kant's *Metaphysic on Morals,* nor indeed from the writings of any well-known moral philosopher, but, just as some people have to worry about the meanings of 'good' and 'duty', so we have to examine data like the above utterance from a number of points of view.

What has the seven-year-old who told us this learned about the basis of moral judgments, and how has she come to learn it? What differences are there among seven-year-old children in such utterances, and can we find correlates of and reasons for these differences? How many ways are there of answering the question posed and why does she give this particular answer, expressed in this linguistic form? What has she learned about language: its functions, forms and semantics? What is there that she had to learn in order to answer such a question?

Fortunately, not all these problems fall within our present frame of reference. We have been trying to develop a theoretical framework which would enable us to classify variations in answers to a range of questions, along with a specification of forms of deviance which might lead to failures in communication. In Chapters 2 and 3 the general theoretical approach is expounded, while our specific applications of the principles outlined are given in detail in Appendix B (Vol. II).

It was expected that children would differ in their capacities and preferences when answering questions, and we wanted to find out whether these differences were systematically linked to other charac-

1

teristics of the children. In particular, Bernstein (see Bernstein, 1970, for the most recent statement, but Bernstein, 1961*b*, for a broader coverage) has suggested that there are social-class differences in child-rearing attitudes and behaviour that should lead to differences in the children's speech. The differences in children's answers to questions which Bernstein's theoretical framework would lead us to expect are given in Chapter 4.

Hence 'social class' has served as the fundamental starting-point for isolating differences in children's language, although attempts have been and are being made to specify both the material and social psychological conditions more immediately relevant. Four sample scripts are contained in Appendix A: mothers of five-year-old children were asked how they would reply to six 'wh'* questions supposing their child had posed them, and one middle- and one working-class mother's answers are presented; two years later their children were asked three of these questions along with twenty-six further ones and transcripts of their answers are also given. The examples provided are not 'typical' in any statistical sense, but neither are they caricatures of extreme cases. A reading of the scripts gives one the impression of certain basic differences in the use made of language, the type of language and the type of information conveyed.

Our problem has been to think up systematic ways of describing answers to questions that will enable us to move away from vague feelings that differences exist to a precise description of what these differences are.

Later in Chapter I we indicate which aspects of which questions were our particular concern and whose answers we studied. We add a brief account of both the applied and pure reasons for the work, showing how it relates to studies of child-rearing practices, education, linguistics, and the behavioural sciences and how it is set within the framework of Bernstein's ideas.

The ways in which we seek to translate the differences illustrated into systematic descriptions will emerge in succeeding chapters, but there has to be an initial discussion of how the eventual frame of reference was delimited and the categories of analysis developed.

2   Answers to which questions

Our interest is not primarily in questions and questioning, but in answers and answering. However, we have found the initial separa-

---

* We use 'wh' to refer to the total set of lexically marked interrogative words and groups: 'who', 'where', 'when', etc. 'How' is included, although its perverse spelling renders it distinct from its bedfellows.

tion and classification of different types of question a necessary preliminary task, because this permits a specification of the type and degree of constraint upon answers. In the course of this account we can also give the reasons for assigning and limiting our interest to the questions chosen.

An attempt to suggest what is involved in questioning and to specify what might count as an answer to a question, as well as a more detailed scheme of classification for both question and answer types, will be undertaken in Chapters 2 and 3, but it is appropriate to mention here the bases upon which we have decided to group and separate questions for analysis and to summarize the nature of our particular involvement with each.

The three bases of (i) *form*, (ii) *content*, and (iii) *context* are not entirely independent of one another: there is overlap between the categories used, but these initial separations may provide a useful framework for description and discussion.

(i) Form

Under considerations of form we are interested in those lexical and grammatical (including grammatically relevant intonational) markers which can be used to group questions. One way of construing these groupings is to treat them as sets (see Fig. 1.1).

(1) The total set of questions, implicit and explicit, may be divided into those which are given verbal expression and those which are not. By verbally expressed questions we mean those which are expressed in language and are explicit, having the linguistic form of an interrogative sentence:

e.g. 'Who are you?', 'Do you come here often?' 'You like it?'

Other verbal expressions, such as 'I wonder who they are', and non-verbal, information-seeking activities are outside our terms of reference, although we recognize that these involve implicit and inferable questions. Only utterances in the interrogative form are included.

(2) Within the set of verbally expressed questions in the interrogative form we can separate open-ended and closed questions. Closed questions offer the possibilities of confirmation or denial as answers and are marked by the predicator preceding the subject or a questioning intonation applied to what otherwise would be a declarative sentence. As these questions may always be and frequently are answered by a simple 'Yes' or 'No', the answers are so constrained

as to be of little linguistic interest. A variant of this form is the disjunctive 'Would you like to go to the cinema *or* stay at home?' The possibilities of choice in answer are again confined, theoretically, to those expressed in the question, so these are likewise of minimal interest. No new lexical items are required in reply to closed questions.

FIG. 1.1 *A diagrammatic representation of question types according to linguistic form*

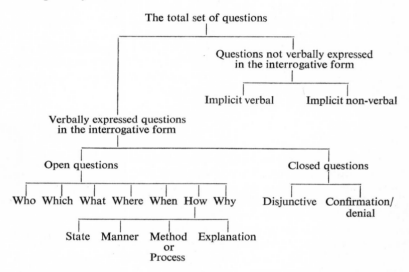

Open-ended questions are introduced by a special grammatical class of interrogative word: 'who', 'which', 'what', 'where', 'when', 'how', and 'why' (rarely 'whence' and 'whither'). For 'where', 'when', 'how', 'why', and occasionally for the others, the predicator precedes the subject, but these positions are reversed when 'who', 'which', or 'what' form part or whole of the nominal group as subject, e.g. 'Who came into the room?' In response to these questions, the answer has to supply new lexical items whose characteristics will depend upon the particular interrogative word used. For example, the answer to 'Who is it?' requires that a person or role is specified, whereas 'Where do you live?' requires the mention of a location. The grammatical form in which the content is expressed also differs with the type of interrogative word, but this is illustrated later.

Our attention is confined to these open-ended questions introduced by interrogative words.

(3) Within the open-ended set of questions we have divided upon the basis of the seven 'wh' words. Compounds like 'Where . . . from?' or 'How much . . . ?' are at present included under their apparent simple source word, viz. 'where' and 'how'. Further groupings, such as 'when' plus 'where' being treated as 'adverbial group' questions, have not been made explicitly, although the range of questions posed to the seven-year-old children implies some such further higher-order grouping.

(4) Within some of these types we can separate different modes of question. This has been done systematically with 'how', for which we distinguish four modes, labelled (1) state, (2) manner, (3) method or process and (4) explanation.

We have chosen to study a small selection of each mode of each interrogative word, with a larger number of 'why' questions. A detailed formal description of types of question is given in Chapters 2 and 3.

(ii) Content

This separation of question types based on form does not exhaust the possibilities for classification, and another significant feature is content. The two aspects of content relevant here are *subject-matter* and *difficulty*. The subject-matter of the question will influence both the form and content of the answer. This is best illustrated with 'why', for which we made a crude separation of 'physical', 'moral' and 'social' matters. With 'why' questions we have, for most purposes, separated out ten modes of answer, some of which are closely associated with the type of content. 38 per cent of the mothers' answers to 'Why do leaves fall off the trees?' made appeals to the regularity of this event, but this mode hardly occurred for the other three 'why' questions. While 68 per cent of the answers to 'Why did his mother cry when Johnny went to hospital?' made direct appeals to emotional states, no other question elicited answers in this category. It therefore seemed useful to take some account of this source of variance. The subdivision on content for 'why' questions accounts for the comparatively larger number of these in the interview schedules.

Difficulty is also relevant in that the answerer's capacity to understand the question and whether he has the information he considers necessary to answer it satisfactorily will determine the answer given. Since it was not our intention to test general knowledge, we chose 'wh' questions to which we expected the children would be able to offer answers.

B

(iii) Context

The third problem area is the context and the ways in which this will constrain the choice of answer given. The aspects of context are many: who the participants are, what the relationship between them is, what assumptions each can make about the other's knowledge and understanding, how much relevant information can be conveyed in non-verbal ways, how much time is available, what medium of language presentation is being used—speech or writing, etc. Questions and answers frequently occur in continuing dialogues with possibilities of guessing and clarification.

We have not looked at the relevance of sociolinguistic variations or dynamic situations, but have taken static snapshots in interview settings. These limitations offer us greater control over the data and comparability across persons, but leave out much of potential interest. The charge that the situations become too 'artificial' can be answered in several ways which will emerge later. As far as possible, the interview settings were two-person situations only, mother and interviewer or child and interviewer. Mothers were interviewed in their own homes; children were interviewed at school. The ambience was generally friendly and relaxed.

3   Whose answers

The bulk of the data is concerned with the answers to 'wh' questions given by five- and seven-year-old children, but a small sample of similar and identical questions were also posed to mothers of five-year-olds. The mothers were asked what they would reply to their children, supposing that their children had asked these questions.

The mothers included in the investigation differed in four ways: their social class, the verbal intelligence test scores and sex of their children and what was labelled their 'communication index'. This was a summary index of their reported manner of dealing with their children's difficult questions and the number of different situations in which they were prepared to talk with their children (Brandis and Henderson, 1970).

The children differed in similar, but not identical ways. For five-year-olds, differences in social class and communication index of mothers and verbal intelligence test scores of children were examined. For seven-year-old girls and boys the major variable was social class, but other variables were included. For boys the relevance of differences in intelligence test scores was examined, while girls were divided into two groups on the basis of the complexity of their speech in a half-hour-long interview at age five. A further variable was participation or non-participation in a 'Use of Language' programme (Gahagan and Gahagan, 1970). A sample of working-class children was allotted to three different treatment groups at age five. One group of children was given twenty minutes a day experience in the use of language as a vehicle for the communication of information about both the physical and social world. They had participated in this programme over five school terms when our questions were given to them. Our control group of children had not participated in such a programme, although their teachers had attended fortnightly seminars at which ways of improving infant teaching were discussed and a number of investigations suggested were subsequently carried out with them by the teachers concerned. The general reasons behind these selections are given below, while the specific reasons are given in the appropriate chapters (5, 6, and 7).

Summary

This overview of the research gives a rough outline of what data have been collected and how we came to select the type of questions posed to mothers and children. The primary concern is in social differences in the form and content of answers to a variety of 'wh' questions. We have yet to explain why the research was conducted.

4 Why conduct the research?

There are both applied (technical) and pure (theoretical) reasons for studying answers to questions. The applied reasons touch upon processes of socialization and education, the pure reasons involve linguistics, developmental social psychology and the intermediate new discipline of sociolinguistics.

The applied reasons are associated with a value judgment about people's relationships to the physical and social world: that it is better that they have a greater understanding and control of their environment. Two major social agencies responsible for the socialization of children are the familial and educational systems. What do these systems make available to children for them to learn, and is there evidence to show that children do exhibit differential learning as a result of exposure to different treatments?

The question-answer dialogue is basic to learning, subsuming at least four problems: to motivate children to ask questions of their environment, to equip them with skills to pose their questions in answerable form, to equip them with skills to find out the answers to these questions and to enable them to assess the validity of their answers. Some principles of a reinforcement theory of learning are often implicit in attempts to achieve these objectives. Curiosity (or avoidance of boredom) is advanced by some psychologists as a basic drive (Berlyne, 1960; Fowler, 1965). Whether or not curiosity is basic or whether it subserves other motives, we can find evidence that animals and children will learn and work to obtain an optimal amount of stimulation from their environment and that the reduction of uncertainty is rewarding (Fowler, op. cit.). Children currently at school are not all as highly motivated to learn as might be considered desirable by those who teach them.

A better understanding of the question-answer situation should facilitate improvements. A specification of the conditions which increase curiosity to an optimal level for learning would render the educational process more satisfactory, satisfying, and productive. It is likely that the provision of certain sorts of answers to children's questions will be relevant to their future questioning behaviour: answers which reduce the uncertainty currently experienced should encourage the production of further questions. The system may well have the perpetual dynamism attributed to the achievement motive by Atkinson (1957), in which the successful attainment of specific standards of excellence will lead to a raising of the levels of aspiration. Analogously, the successful discovery of answers to questions may increase the number of questions posed.

For maximally efficient functioning, a command of language will be an essential feature of the other three conditions of learning mentioned: the capacities to formulate questions appropriately, to know what might count as a valid answer and to know how to find out answers. The role of language will become more important with increasing age if a person is to become and remain a full participant in the culture of his society and that society is a complex urban one.

Applied to individuals and social groups in our society, the problem is that the currently offered answers to their questions may not be such as to increase their understanding and control of their environment, and that part of the failure of certain groups to grasp the educational opportunities apparently available to them may derive from the consequences of a negative feedback loop in which questions are given unsatisfying answers, thereby discouraging further questioning. On the other hand, the provision of satisfying answers under appropriate conditions could enable the socializing agents, primarily teachers and mothers to move to a position where they had only to direct and guide a child's learning, rather than arouse and maintain his motivation as well.

It is hoped that a description of the relationships between the various strategies and tactics adopted by different mothers and the correlated differences in the performance of their children may be of some use to the teachers and mothers who encounter young children, so that the consequences of different ways of handling children's questions can be better appreciated.

The purity of pure sciences inheres not in their superiority, but in their concern with taxonomy and theory. They try to describe and explain rather than to control or predict, except where these latter activities are relevant to theoretical problems. This particular study impinges on the several disciplines already mentioned.

The relevance to *linguistics* is in description rather than in explanation. We attempt to specify the linguistic features of questions and their answers, attending to both similarities and differences across the varieties of each. We try to expose some of the principles governing the replacement of elements and the reorganization of structure necessary to convert question forms into their correlative answer forms. Where a range of options is open to the answerer, we have attempted to classify these and to note the grammatical and lexical markers of each.

Four aspects of *developmental social psychology* are involved. Although the sampling of mothers' and children's answers to questions is neither random nor based on any quota system to provide estimates of the modal behaviour of particular age or sex groups, the data do present examples of answers which could be a guide for normative studies. We also gain some appreciation of levels of difficulty and conceptualization both at the upper and lower limits: all our five-year-old children had an understanding of what questions and answers are and roughly what sort of answer is acceptable to which kind of question, although their capacity to deal adequately with the 'why' questions was limited. The answers of the seven-year-olds often referred only to a particular concrete example or a part of the matter covered by the question and their first utterance often could not be developed further.

This can be linked to the cognitive-developmentalist approach to child development. Our study has relevance to Piaget's early studies of moral judgment (Piaget, 1932) and his concern with the child's understanding of causality (Piaget, 1930) as well as the alleged switch from egocentric to sociocentric speech (Piaget, 1926). Our data raise the question of how far the developmental sequences of conceptions of causality and morality suggested by Piaget and elaborated by Kohlberg (1969) may be modified by verbal interaction, which in turn may encourage an orientation towards the physical world and problems of morality, other than those mentioned by him.

We also add to the number of studies illustrating social-class differences in the verbal behaviour of children and attempt to show the relationships to the behaviour of mothers. Although there are similarities to those studies which seek simply to specify qualitative and quantitative linguistic differences in children (e.g. Irwin, 1948; Templin, 1957), to those which have a more general concern about social-class differences in child-rearing (see Bronfenbrenner, 1958, for a review), and to those concerned with the structure and dynamics of the whole complex of parent-child interaction (see Becker, 1964, and Clausen, 1964, for reviews), our closest links are to those studies particularly interested in social-class differences in parental behaviour as these are related to language differences in children (e.g. Hess and Shipman, 1967; Deutsch, 1967). The most comprehensive current review of this field is by Cazden (1966).

Sociolinguistics is a new area of inquiry for the social sciences. A recent prescription for its domain from Hymes (1967, p.13) is:

> There must be a study of speaking that seeks to determine the native system and theory of speaking: whose aim is to describe the communicative competence that enables a member of the community to know when to speak and when to remain silent, which code to use, when, where and to whom, etc. In considering what form sociolinguistic description might take, . . . one needs to *see* data as the interaction of language and social setting.

Ervin-Tripp (1969) states that it is useful in sociolinguistics to distinguish between three types of rules: alternation, sequence, and co-occurrence. Problems of alternation are exemplified by the range of forms from which choices can be made and the determinants of the choices made. Shall I address her as Dr Tripp, Professor Tripp, Mrs Tripp, Susan, Sue, darling, etc.? Answers to 'wh' questions do involve selections between alternatives. Our taxonomic scheme seeks to specify these (Chapters 2 and 3), while our empirical work goes some way to establishing patterns of differential usage of these options by different subgroups of children. Problems of sequence arise from the fact that events have a temporal structure, necessary or normative, and where speech is involved in this activity it should be possible to specify sequences, e.g. in English conversation we say or are likely to say 'Hallo, Mr Smith!' rather than 'Mr Smith. Hallo!' and we are under considerable constraint to start conversations with 'Hallo!' and finish them with 'Goodbye!' rather than to use these greetings in reverse order. We have not investigated sequence rules, partly because we have generally used a single answer to a single question situation. Rules of co-occurrence refer to the limitations of choice at all linguistic levels as defined by the total linguistic and non-linguistic context. Ervin-Tripp (op. cit., p.38) cites the example: 'How's it going, Your Eminence? Centrifuging O.K.? Also have you been analyzin' whatch' unnertook t'achieve?' As she states, this mythical remark conjures up an implausible episode in the English-speaking biochemistry lab. of the Vatican. Our contribution to 'what goes with what' in answer to 'wh' questions is developed in Volume II, although not from the actual linguistic perspective that Ervin-Tripp has in mind.

Some of these links arise by accident rather than design, especially for example, with the Ervin-Tripp contribution, which post-dates our inquiries. By design, our work was set within the theoretical framework developed by Bernstein about the location, transmission, functions and structure of what he has called 'restricted' codes. The particular restricted code is that to which the members of the lower working class in contemporary British society may be confined, and originally the confinement to this code was proposed to be an important determinant of the under-achievement of this social group in the educational system (Bernstein, 1959). The lower working class do under-achieve educationally in many respects: compared with their middle-class peers, they are less likely to enter higher education, they are more likely to leave grammar or secondary modern schools earlier, they are less likely to be selected for grammar schools, they find themselves in the lower streams of all schools and perform less well in these (see Central Advisory Council for Education (England): 1954, 1959, 1963a, 1963b, 1966; Morton-Williams and Finch, 1968, or Douglas, 1964; Vernon, 1969; Wiseman, 1964, for more easily read summaries of aspects of these differences).

A specification of the role working-class language plays in the total pattern of the determinants of their depressed educational performance cannot be given, although it is not difficult to see how the characteristics of the restricted code described by Bernstein (1961a) would limit their educability.

Perhaps the simplest illustration of this point can be made by posing questions about the functions of language, questions too seldom posed for a variety of reasons (Robinson, 1970a). What do we use language for? It is unfashionable nowadays to generate lists, but one nine-year-old (Paul Rackstraw) had little difficulty in thinking up several: to give messages, to communicate to your friend what you know, to explain things, to tell someone off, to ask permission. We cannot improve greatly on this, although we hope to eventually (Robinson, 1970b): to ask for or give knowledge or beliefs about the physical and social world external to oneself and report on 'private' states (referential function), often by making statements or posing questions; to control other people's behaviour, often by issuing commands; to relieve tensions by exclaiming; to order one's own non-verbal behaviour; to attract or retain attention; to joke and recite or create poetry; to conform to social norms; to identify one's status; to define the role relationship between speaker and listener; to teach someone else the language.

Such a classification purports neither to be exhaustive nor satisfactory, but it does enable us to illustrate important differences. We would argue that the educational system is most directly concerned with the referential function: the assimilation of knowledge about the physical and social world in which we live, and by 'knowledge' we intend not only 'facts', but problem posing and solving, learning to learn, skills and other activities often inappropriately treated as distinct from 'knowledge'. The basis of evaluation for statements made about the world is that of truth or falsity, so that the language used for such a function has always to be checked for its correspondence to the features of the non-verbal world about which it is used to comment. Bernstein's 'elaborated' code has this referential function, but not only does the code's characteristics require that it bear a correspondence to the non-verbal world, its users are oriented towards the use of language as the major means of intra- and inter-individual communication and for the processing of such information.

The restricted code of the lower working class is supposed to serve primarily social functions: to define the nature of the social relationship between speaker and listener, e.g. mother, mate, son, boss, employee, etc., exemplified by rights to command, jokes, etc. Hence a speaker of such a code is not concerned with the referential function and is not oriented towards its exploitation for the assimilation and transmission of true or false propositions about the world.

The linguistic structures of the codes differ, being adapted to the particular functions they serve. Hence this restricted code is not conducive to educational success: its user is not oriented to the referential function of language, and the structures and the rules governing their usage are inappropriate for easy transfer.

Evidence for the validity of Bernstein's position is accumulating, while the theoretical model has been developed and refined (Bernstein, 1970).

The features of this theory most relevant to ways of answering 'wh' questions and the predictions we derive from these are in Chapter 4.

Chapter 2 The question-answer exchange

Introduction

The gentle and general description of the problems posed and the reasons for investigating them must eventually give way to a more thorough examination of the linguistic and behavioural features relevant to the question-answer exchange. We have looked at the map, decided where we want to go, chosen a route and noted some salient features of the journey. In this chapter we begin to move. Our starting-point might be thought of as the heart of London on a foggy evening in the rush hour. Towards the end of the chapter we arrive in the suburbs and eventually hit the open countryside, through which we can travel with greater speed and ease in Chapter 3.

We begin with a delimitation of the frame of reference and then attempt to clarify the question-answer situation under twelve headings in this chapter. In Chapter 3 the described scheme for the analysis of answers is elaborated and illustrated with particular examples.

In presenting the scheme of analysis we are faced with a choice between trying to offer a system of general application suitable for all answers to all 'wh' questions and confining ourselves to our own particular problems. The resultant compromise does not stem from indecisiveness. The data we had to work with imposed certain restrictions upon the extent to which the scheme could be claimed to have universal applicability. For the most part, the answers we examined were short, single answers given by a limited sample of subjects in a limited range of situations—and the questions were not genuine requests for information, but stimuli presented by an experimenter.

These constraints do not invalidate the scheme, but do leave it open to amendment and supplementation. One of the most serious constraints is to treat the question-answer exchange as an isolated and encapsulated event when it is often part of an extended interaction. When in Chapter 3 we mention alternative ways of posing the 'same' question, these are not necessarily simple equivalents;

sometimes they are demands for more precision in an answer or attempts to restrict the choice of mode acceptable as an answer. Some of the difficulties encountered in describing answers to 'wh' questions arise from the vagueness of the interrogative words themselves, but in conversational situations this vagueness can be eradicated by further question-answer sequences. The problems apply to both questioner and answerer. The questioner poses a problem, but he has some knowledge in the associated area of the question. The answer which is optimally efficient, that reduces uncertainty or ignorance most economically, could be defined, given the present state of knowledge and belief of the questioner and answerer and what is known about the problem itself. Departures from maximal efficiency can take several forms: the problem may be posed in inadequate linguistic terms, the answerer can overestimate or under-estimate the knowledge of the questioner, etc. If a mismatch occurs there are tactics available for salvaging the situation. For ambiguous questions the answerer can demand clarification, either general, e.g. 'What do you mean?' or specific, 'Do you want to know his name or what his job is?' If the answerer guesses and resolves the ambiguity or vagueness wrongly, the questioner can render his inquiry more precise. Some of the ways in which this can be done are given in Chapter 3.

It is possible that in naturally occurring conversations some minimal effort principle applies. A questioner trades a vagueness and ambiguity for speed and brevity; an answerer risks presuppositions for similar reasons. If a mismatch is seen to occur, successive tactical exchanges home on to a mutually acceptable solution.

The ambiguity and vagueness probably serve as defences against rigidity. Variations in context or shared knowledge and belief require, for average optimal efficiency, that it is better to have approximations with successive refinements than over-elaboration and specificity. The flexibility allows a marriage of economy of effort and completeness of answering, while avoiding the evolutionary dead-end of over-specialization, resulting in a lack of means of adaptation to changes in the environment.

If these suggestions are valid, a search for specifications of appropriateness, completeness and presupposition at the levels of context, mode, grammar and lexis is warranted, not by an expectation that precise specifications are available to be discovered, but because such an approach may clarify what lies at the heart of question-answer situations. The clarification should facilitate later descriptions of successful and unsuccessful interchanges and indicate ways of eliminating failures in communication. To deal with single answers to single questions may be a useful starting-point.

We treat the issues involved under a succession of headings:

(1) *Questions and questioning*
     (i) Prerequisites of questioning
    (ii) Types of questions
   (iii) The linguistic forms of questions
  (iii*a*) Similarities and differences in the form of open and closed questions
  (iii*b*) Subcategories of open questions
   (iv) Referential categories for questions
    (v) The scope of questioning

(2) *Answers and answering*
   (vi) Problems of definition
  (vii) Linguistic criteria of answers with summary

(3) *A scheme for the description of answers*
 (viii) Appropriateness, completeness and presupposition
   (ix) Core, concordance and residue
    (x) Context
  (x*a*) Participants, register (field, role, formality, medium)
  (x*b*) Appropriateness, completeness, presupposition
  (xi) Mode: appropriateness, completeness
 (xii) Form: grammar and lexis – appropriateness, completeness, presupposition

1   Questions and questioning

Since the primary concern is with answering rather than questioning behaviour, questions are only examined sufficiently to ascertain how they function to elicit answers of various kinds and how they relate to these answers.

Hence we are not concerned with what prompts people to ask questions except in so far as this may influence the acceptability of different answers. Questioning may serve a variety of functions. To reduce uncertainty about the matter explicitly referred to in the question might be viewed as a basic function, although attempts to obtain goods and services may be the first to appear in children. But questioning can also be used to obtain or retain attention, to test authority, to register a protest, to evoke embarrassment or other emotional states, to prevent an uncomfortable silence or as a rhetorical device. We do not attempt to develop ways of finding out which functions particular questions are serving. Our conceptual analysis treats questioning at its face value as an activity intended to reduce uncertainty about the subject-matter presented in a question. Situational determinants of questioning are taken as given, and individual or social differences in the incidence or type of questions asked are also not our present problem.

The difficulty of many problem-solving situations, in science as well as 'Twenty Questions', is often supposed to be mainly overcome once pertinent rather than irrelevant questions are asked or once optimal interrogation strategies have been devised. Alas! these considerations of questioning in sequential problem-solving are also excluded from consideration.

What is left is questioning stripped of its complexity, but this initial simplification may make the task of definition easier.

(i) The prerequisites of questioning

Questioning is a behavioural activity manifestly related to the acquisition of knowledge. The existence of the possibility of questioning seems to depend upon two conditions: (1) a gap in a framework of knowledge or belief, and (2) the availability of alternatives for filling that gap.

(1) Regardless of whether the answer is already known to the questioner or not, the possibility of questioning requires that he has (a) a framework of knowledge and belief, and (b) either has a gap in this framework or can conceive of one.

The parameters of a particular framework are defined by a questioner when he specifies the size and function of the gap.

Example: A person called John Smith has put a book on a table. This event, or my imagining this event, offers me an opportunity to conceive questions about it. I may inquire, 'Who put a book on a table?' thus revealing a knowledge or belief about a book which was put on a table (by someone). 'John Smith' can now be integrated into that framework of knowledge. Knowledge about a book having been put on a table can stand alone. It only becomes incomplete when I enlarge my framework of thinking to demand an identification of the implied actor. Other questions might concern: what John Smith did, the framework of knowledge being that John Smith is an actor in some situation; or in what location the book was put, knowing or believing that it was put somewhere. I may arrive at a complete knowledge of the event as expressed in 'John Smith put a book on a table', yet I can still go on to demand an explanation for this action, a specification of the manner in which it was done, the time it took place, a more precise identification of the table, the name of the book, and so on, each time using the knowledge I have about the event and about what is implied by the event and of relevant categories impinging upon the event to construct a new framework with new gaps to be filled.

(2) The second prerequisite of questioning is that of holding a set of possible ideas as answers not all of which empirically are, or even logically could be, true. A question is posed signifying a gap (1) which may be filled by one or more from a set of possible entries. If the questioning person could not conceive of the possibility of an entry different from that presently given, there could not be a question. This is not to say that the alternative can be specified, but only that any present entry is capable of being denied.

(ii) Types of questions

In Chapter 1 it was suggested that questions fall into two broad, contrasting types:

Type 1. 'Open', information-seeking This type of question most clearly exemplifies prerequisite (1), since it functions to discover information relevant to filling gaps in a framework of knowledge. One linguistic expression of such a question is 'What is X?' An assumption is made that 'X' is something characterizable by the relative pronoun 'what', i.e. an object, substance, position, or process which can be referred to by a substantive. The demand is for a specification of its nature.

Of course, the presumed truth value of the information already given in the question can be rejected, e.g. 'Who took that?' 'Nobody.' It could be argued that the assumption of the question being invalid should have been anticipated by a prior investigatory Type 2 question, e.g. 'Did anybody take that?'

Type 2. 'Closed', confirmation/denial-seeking The second prerequisite involves the conception of a set of statements at least one of which may be false. This type of question demands that a truth value be assigned to a statement. A closed set binary decision is required, as opposed to the more open set of choices offered by a Type 1 question. If the question consists of a series of statements or offers more than one alternative, a succession of binary decisions may be required. The linguistic expression of such a question might take the form: 'Is X Y?' Once the existence or meaningfulness of 'X' is presumed, then the predication of it as 'Y' may be either confirmed or denied.

These two types of questioning do not imply different subject-matters of interest. It could be argued that they are polar extremes along a dimension of minimal to maximal constraint. Questions like

'You would agree that the blue one is prettier, wouldn't you?' appear to offer a somewhat biased binary choice, but husbands advising their wives when out shopping might not feel that they are being given any discretion in the form and content of their reply. At the other extreme, 'why' questions allow a very wide range of choice, but perhaps each type could also be viewed as reducible to the other. The confirmation/denial question type could be made redundant by reducing the prior assumptions of the question, e.g. 'Who took the book?' might obtain the same information as 'Did X take the book?'; the open version could serve an equivalent function. Similarly, the information-seeking Type 1 question could be rendered redundant if all alternative possible answers and their potential truth values could be conveniently specified and converted to binary decisions. If all possible answers to 'What is X?' were listed, a succession of 'Is X Y?' questions, where 'Y' takes all possible values, should lead to a solution.

The choice of form will be multiply determined, but, all else being equal, the probability of obtaining a quick, useful closure of the knowledge gap is greater, it would seem, the nearer to the open end of the dimension the question can be formulated.

It might also be argued that there is an intermediate level of constraint which offers a multiple choice from a defined set of possibilities. Such alternatives may be exclusive, but not through being empirically or logically opposite. The assumption is that at least one will be given a truth value different from the others, e.g. 'Did you walk to work this morning or did you come by bus?' These can be generalized, 'How did you come to work this morning?' or reduced to a succession of binary decisions, 'Did you walk to work this morning?'

It may seem odd to elect for a typology when a continuous dimension can be conceived and perhaps realized. Our decision to do so can make an appeal to what people actually do: 'wh' questions are frequently not reduced to a finite set of binary choices and confirmation/denial questions are not necessarily posed in a more general manner. For empirical purposes, it is therefore a reasonable decision to use the two types rather than the continuum; a variable from which two values take up most of the cases may be better treated as discontinuous, at least for the purposes of social science.

(iii) The linguistic forms of questions

The two types of question have each what might be called their normal form of linguistic expression in interrogative clauses. Under some circumstances, it might be sensible to include expressions representing features central to the concept of question, viz. to obtain information or to confirm or deny, but which are not expressed in the interrogative form, e.g. 'Let's see how X works', 'Tell me whether X is true'. These imperative demands could be construed as demands for answers to questions whose interrogative forms are readily made overt: 'Let's see the answer to the question, "How do you work X?"' and 'Tell me the answer to the question, "Is X true?"'

Certain declarative forms of statements can also function as questions, e.g. 'I should like to know the meaning of this', 'I wonder if it has any meaning'. These examples manifest the two prerequisites of questioning cited above. Independent of context, however, they may be better treated as statements of which the major theme is the actor's uncertainty.

The normal forms of the two types have both similarities and differences.

(a) SIMILARITIES AND DIFFERENCES IN FORM FOR OPEN AND CLOSED QUESTIONS

Type 1: *Open, information-seeking*	*Type 2:* *Closed, confirmation/denial-seeking*
At least clause rank. Where the interrogative group is not of the class 'nominal', predicator precedes subject. 'Wh' interrogative marker at word or group rank. In the unmarked form the interrogative marker is the first word in the clause.	At least clause rank. *Either* Predicator precedes subject. *Or* Rising intonation at the end of the utterance (Jones, 1956, tune 2). When predicator precedes subject the verb or the auxiliary 'do' is the first word in the clause.
If the substance is phonic (oral questions), there is a normal intonation pattern (Jones, 1956, tune 1). If the substance is graphic (written questions), '?' is used at the end.	If the substance is phonic, there is a normal intonation pattern (Jones, 1956, tune 2, for unmodified, and tune 2+1 for disjunctives). If the substance is graphic, '?' is used at the end.

(b) SUBCATEGORIES OF OPEN QUESTIONS

Open questions may be divided into types on the basis of the different interrogative markers used, and we may differentiate between 'who', 'which', 'where', 'when', 'what', 'how' and 'why' questions. This division of open questions enables a specification of the particular linguistic constraints that a given question type exercises on potential answers.

'How' questions are more complicated than others in that they appear to divide into four distinct types or 'modes' which have linguistic markers in their associated answers (see Chapter I). Mode 1 of 'how' is concerned with state or adjectival description and is marked by an ascriptive verb demanding an intensive complement, e.g. 'How are you?', 'How long is the wall?' Mode 2 expresses manner and demands an adverbial group, e.g. 'How did it go?, 'How well do you ski?' Mode 3 asks for a specification of a process or method which may be supplied by a series of free clauses or by an adverbial group introduced by an agentive marker like 'by' or 'with', e.g. 'How do you ride a bicycle?' Mode 4 is the theme predicated type which asks for an explanation that may take many forms, e.g. 'How is it that John always gets here first?'

(iv) Referential categories for open questions

It may be possible to regard the different subcategories of questions defined by their interrogative words or groups as normally representing referential categories within which information may be sought. A small set of interrogatives appears to have a specifying function within the referential categories normally represented by other words or groups.

We have sought to reduce the number of referential categories to a minimum by making each as inclusive as possible. The list which emerges is as follows:

Category	Subcategories	Normal interrogative groups
1 Identification	(a) Personal object	Who
	(b) Impersonal object	What
	(c) Action	What (+ doing, happening, etc.)
2 Definition		What (+ is/are)
3 Description (non-state)		What like, What about
4 Placing	(a) Time	When
	(b) Space	Where
5 Explanation	(a) Categorization	Why
	(b) Effect	Why
	(c) Cause	Why, how (4)
6 Process		How (3)
7 Degree		How (1), how (2) (+ relevant dimension)
8 State		How (1)
9 Kind		Which (+ noun)
10 Manner		How (2)

The interrogative markers which serve to specify and classify are 'what' and 'which'. They can act within the other categories to specify the sort of answer required, '**At** what time did he come?' This asks for the same sort of answer as that required by a 'when' time-placing question prescribing the mode of answer (p. 59). There are also instances of groups operating within other groups, e.g. 'How long ago was the war?' Time-placing is the background category, degree the surface concern. This specifies the mode of answer (for a 'when' question), just as the former example does.

Closed confirmation/denial questions can operate within any of the groups, e.g. (Identification) 'Is this a knife?' (Explanation) 'Did you do it for my sake?'

(v) The scope of questioning

The systematic cognitive acquisition of knowledge (systematic and cognitive as opposed to random impressions received or the emotional sort of 'connaître' knowledge by direct experience) is the result of questions being explicitly or implicitly posed.

The questioner and answerer may be the same person, as in the case when I wonder where some object is. I can form the relevant question in my mind which might be represented, 'Where is it?', the assumption being that it is somewhere, and I can then test various hypotheses about its location, 'Is it here?' by looking in various places. The use of language and the freedom it gives for conceiving of events beyond our normal range of present experience may sometimes result in a combination of words which cannot relate together to give any feasible structural framework. What has been presupposed implicitly in the foregoing sections is that questions are 'answerable' at both the linguistic and conceptual levels. This does not mean that the assumptions of the question have to be valid or that answers have to be empirically true, but that the 'question' as a whole must 'mean' something and be more than a linguistic form: non-example, 'Who is the radio?'

The non-example ascribes personality to an inanimate object, thus producing a semantic anomaly (Katz and Fodor, 1963), which may be labelled either 'an improper question' or 'a non-question'. The difficulty in deciding what status to ascribe to certain linguistic expressions which look like questions is paralleled in the difficulty which may be encountered when judging whether a response constitutes an answer or not. This is our next problem.

c

2 Answers and answering

(vi) Problems of definition

Answers will have to be examined both as acts of behaviour within the framework of the behavioural sciences and as verbal utterances of interest to linguistics, but it may be useful to make some general introductory remarks. Already the distinction has been made between questioning as an activity and the linguistic forms in which this may be expressed. With answers it seems necessary to define them in relation to questions: answers are responses to questions. Although non-verbal responses may be given to many questions, we are concerned only with verbal responses. Not all categories of utterance are normally considered suitable as answers to questions. If we distinguish between statements, questions, commands and exclamations, then answers are statements, although other categories of reply and interchange may intervene between the initial question and the answer, but we are not concerned with such failures to hear, attempts to clarify, etc. Normatively then, answers are statements occurring in response to questions. In one sense, all statements may be seen as answers to potential questions, in that it is possible to invent questions to which given statements could be answers; for, just as the generation of questions presupposes the creation or acceptance of gaps in frameworks of knowledge and belief, so statements can be conceptualized as gap-fillers within possible frameworks.

At this stage no more will be said about answers *per se*, but we can ask what qualifies a particular statement to be treated as an answer to a particular question. We have suggested a variety of responses to a question which would not qualify as answers, such as non-verbal behaviour, exclamations, questions and commands, but other non-qualifying responses, such as an explicit refusal to answer, may occur. If the response conveys information in a statement, it still may not be treated by the questioner as an answer, for he may reply, 'You have not answered my question', 'I already know that,' 'That's no answer'. We are not concerned about games involving deception, evasion or subterfuge, but similar retorts could also be made when the answerer believes he has answered the question.

Hence, we may have to consider the questioner's expectations as well as the answerer's intention and understanding of the concept 'answer' to produce a satisfactory behavioural definition of answer, where 'satisfactory' involves as close an approximation to common usage as is consistent with conceptual clarity. We need to explore therefore how far the linguistic form and content of possible answers to questions can be of use in this.

(vii) The linguistic criteria of answers

We have already located the normal form of the question in an interrogative clause structure, with the reservation that other means of posing questions exist. The normal form of an answer is minimally a statement expressed in a declarative clause structure in which the subject precedes the predicator, although again informative replies may take on other forms, e.g. 'What shall I do with this piece of string?' 'What do you normally do with things which are of no more use?' Although in this instance a further question is posed, there is an assumption that the questioner will know the answer to it now that the string has been allocated to the category of useless objects. Perhaps it would be useful to maintain that the question cannot truly be said to be answered before the questioner has made the necessary inference, which could now be expressed as a statement. This would mean that such replies could be treated as non-answers from which answers may be derived without further questioning.

These general grammatical criteria for examining replies to questions can be supplemented by a consideration of the lexical relations between questions and responses. For a response to be an answer there must be *lexical continuity* between it and the question. This continuity may be explicit or presupposed, as in the case of answers like 'Yes' to confirmation/denial questions in which the whole lexical content of the question is presupposed.

Summary procedure for evaluating whether a response is an answer

The decision as to whether or not a response is to be regarded as an answer may be made by reference to a series of ordered binary choices (i.e. closed questions) for which a 'Yes' answer permits a progression to the next question:

(1) Has a question been posed?
(2) Was it posed in a linguistic form?
(3) Was this form the interrogative?

If these three are true, than we may proceed to look for an answer:

(4) Has the question been received by somebody from whom an answer would be acceptable?
(5) Has such a person made some acknowledgment of having received the question?

(6) Has he supplied some linguistic expression as a result of having received the question?
(7) Does the linguistic expression convey a statement?
(8) Is the statement *not* a refusal to answer?
(9) Is the statement expressed in at least one declarative clause?
(10) Is there some lexical continuity with the question in terms of 'collocation' or 'set' (p. 39)?

If all these are true, then an answer can be said to have been given, although we might add one further question, viz.:

(11) Can the statement given reasonably be understood as functioning within the same referential category as the question?

However, since the referential categories are as yet new and have not undergone any form of testing, we hesitate to apply such a criterion for the exclusion of responses as answers.

The criteria we have used for separating answers from non-answers are as follows:

Behaviourally, an answer must

(1) follow in time an interrogatively posed question;
(2) be given by a person who has received the question;
(3) be expressed in language.

Formally, an answer must

(1) consist of at least one declarative clause;
(2) have lexical continuity with the question.

Contextually, an answer must

(1) convey a statement,
(2) not consist of a refusal to answer,

and (probably)

(3) be able to function within the same referential category as the question.

As we proceed to apply these criteria to empirical data, a rule will occasionally be waived, e.g. we may judge it more informative to treat a response as an answer so that we may analyse it further, rather than to record it simply as a non-answer. Such considerations are most likely to apply within form, for instance, when a statement can be inferred from an interrogative form. Also, when the absence of lexical continuity makes the response seem unconnected to the question, we choose to call it an irrelevant *answer* rather than a non-answer.

3   A scheme for the description of answers

Having decided what will count as an answer, we can proceed to consider the problems associated with describing answers. We shall do this under three headings: context, mode and form. At these three levels we are concerned with three aspects: appropriateness, completeness and presupposition. Three answer areas, core, concordance and residue, are separated for the description of appropriateness and completeness at the levels of context and form. Some definition of these three aspects and three answer areas seems necessary before we move on to discuss the three levels and how they operate within them.

(viii) Appropriateness, completeness and presupposition

Appropriateness means something like 'correct', either in terms of correspondence with the real world (contextual) or of grammatical and lexical acceptability (formal) or of the suitability of the 'type' of information content that is given (mode).

Completeness is the aspect concerned with how much is given or omitted in a reply. This may be in terms of information items (contextual), of grammatical elements and lexical precision (formal), or of the number of different modes used (mode).

Presupposition is relevant to what is given or not given in the answer in the light of what is being, will be, or has already been given elsewhere. This may be in terms of the information that is presumed to be known (contextual). It may be in terms of 'necessary' elements of grammatical structure not given in the answer because they are in the question, and expounded lexical identification of objects or actions not given in the answer because reference is made back to the specific identifications within the question by the use of substitute words, e.g. pronouns (formal). Presupposition of mode assumes that a certain type of information is required or not required in a given situation.

(ix) Core, concordance and residue

Answers are also divided into three areas for the application of these aspects to the different levels. This division does not apply to mode or presupposition in that all modes are necessarily core features, lexical presupposition is a feature of concordance, and grammatical presupposition may be used to isolate the grammatical core rather than operating within any area. It does seem to be relevant for assessing appropriateness and completeness within context and form. The three areas are (i) the *core* area of the answer, (ii) the *concordant* area of the answer, and (iii) the *residual* area of the answer. Brief definition only will be given at present. Their significance will emerge in the course of the description of formal and contextual appropriateness and completeness.

(1) The 'core' area is the area of specifically required linguistic and informational items for an answer in a particular mode to a particular question type posed in a particular question mode (where relevant).

(2) The 'concordant' area is the area of required systemic, lexical and information parallels to the question.

(3) The 'residual' area is what is not covered under (1) and (2) and can be treated as any utterance rather than as an answer to a particular question.

It must be realized that the answer areas are conceptual areas not strictly locatable in space, although we do define instances of lexical appropriateness and completeness as core features or other, simply according to whether they are located within those grammatical structures which form a *grammatically appropriate core*.

Not all the areas will be relevant for both aspects at the two levels to which they apply. In the studies which we shall later go on to describe, not all the possible separations were made, while there were others made which did not follow this scheme. We will attempt now to give a description of the levels of context, mode and form and to show in what way the three aspects and areas fit into a more total picture of the question-answer situation.

(x) Context

We have seen (p. 16) that the potential for meaningful questioning inheres in the conceptions we are able to have about any universe we choose to define as such. The way in which questioning functions in the particular case will depend upon certain relevant features in the questioner and his environment.

The linguistic interlevel of context relates items at the level of form to items of situation in order to obtain contextual meaning (Ellis, 1966). According to Ellis, contextual meaning may refer to one of two things:

(1) *potential contextual meaning*, which is the range of possible contextual meanings of an item considered in abstraction from any text.

(2) *instantial contextual meaning*, which is the actual meaning for a given instance of occurrence in a given place of a given text in a given situation.

When a particular unit of form (minimally a sentence) is related to the situation, one arrives at the instantial meaning. Thus when we take an interrogative sentence which has been given, and bring to bear all those situational features relevant to the understanding of its unique meaning, we can see how as a question it may function for obtaining an answer. A complete categorization of situational features which would thoroughly disambiguate any sentence is not at present available, and may well be a task of infinite and therefore impossible proportions. It may be, however, that for our present purpose we will be able to make use of some of the rather ill-defined categories belonging to the area of contextual meaning.

(a) PARTICIPANTS AND REGISTER

Of some importance will be the *participant* features, that is the relevant features of performer and addressee (questioner and intended answerer), i.e. 'those actively determining the utterance or being relevantly affected by it'. The participants each possess a language (a feature of what is called 'the wider situation') with its socially and locally determined characteristics, from which selection is made more or less according to the demands of the immediate situation. In other words, they possess an idiolect consisting of a series of *registers* (language according to use rather than user).

Register Let us remember that we are at present interested chiefly in how a given question functions to obtain an answer of a particular description. We can look at the form of the question and note the variety of different meanings it might have for an addressee who is to respond to it. We can then look at the situation in which it was uttered for more clues as to how it might be interpreted and how it might be answered. This may look like a long and complicated task. Few people in making answers actually appear to consider all possible interpretations other than the one they choose and which leads them to make the particular utterance that they do. This is because they are 'in the situation' and are quickly aware of the particular features which are relevant for interpretation. They have learnt from past experience with similar questions in similar situations that certain answers may be given. That is, they have already categorized more or less finally the features relevant to their behaviour. This does not mean that they are aware of all possibilities in all situations. Differences in the sorts of language used for different purposes may be more or less salient for an answerer. The context of the question, linguistic and situational features may be more or less heeded. The perceived intentions of the questioner, his present state of knowledge and his orientations may influence an answerer to a greater or lesser degree.

The *scales* of register are a feature of form; a discussion of them will show how situational features can influence form, and how these formal-language differences can make differences at the level of situation salient. It must be noted that when we apply these scales to our own purposes, we may not represent them very fully and may distort their authors' original intention (Halliday, McIntosh and Strevens, 1964).

Field is the scale of which the situational determinants are found in the subject-matter of the utterance. It is concerned with the way in which speech refers to selected features of the universe.

'By thesis is meant the event, process, action or state of affairs to which the utterance refers' (Ellis, 1966, p. 84). Our proposed referential categories of questioning mentioned above (p. 20) may serve to describe ways of focusing upon a thesis through the use of interrogative words.

Role formally specifies the social function, whether it be conversational, literary, instructional or whatever.

Formality specifies the degree of intimacy or social distance between participants.

Mode or *medium* (as we shall call it) specifies those formal features effected by the way in which a message is transmitted and how much feedback is possible, the form of written speech differing from that which is tape-recorded, broadcast, televised, and so on. Finally, the *residual* scale, which has been posited by Ure (unpublished manuscript), occurs within text only and relates to individual style.

How can these be usefully applied to our eventual analysis of answers? We have noticed how the different interrogative words can specify different referential categories. This is part of *field*. Within field also we find differences of speech relating to different subject-matter. We might choose to categorize the subject-matter as *technical*, and we would then talk about it differently from the way we would talk about *non-technical* matter. The lexical items and grammatical structures will be different for geography and physics. A broad separation into *scientific* and *non-scientific* with their different formal correlates may be useful for certain purposes. When a question is asked we shall be able to describe the language used in terms of some category or categories of field. One might ask a question in philosophy, for instance, or a question about everyday happenings, a question about meteorology or one about the weather—and the person answering is expected to reply within the constraints of the language associated with the particular type of subject-matter. He is therefore required to understand the particular lexical items used in the question in the particular way they are used. He should understand the particular use of grammar and be able himself to produce the lexical collocates of the words in the question and combine them in the acceptable way.

Questions function to elicit answers; answers to reduce the gap in knowledge indicated by the question. This is quite independent of the motivation or desires of the participants in the process, viz. questioner and answerer. Question posing and answering can be considered a formal exercise which specifies gaps in a conceptual framework and then fills them in. The scale of register *role* relates speech to the social situation in such a way as to separate the different functions of questions, which are themselves related directly or indirectly to purposes and intentions. In an academic examination, for example, a question is often intended to direct the attention of the examinee to a particular area of his supposed knowledge and requires that he discuss all the information he considers relevant in the limited time available, e.g. Is Darwin's theory of evolution true? In a conversation, however, the same question may be intended to make a second person talk for a certain short amount of time. The response which follows may be fairly uninformative with respect to the subject-matter of the question and yet satisfy the situational requirements as adequately as any other. If full details were given about a particular content, this might be dysfunctional to conversation as such, turning it into something more like a lecture or a monologue. There is an obvious difference in the amount of uninterrupted speech required for these different roles. There will be other characteristics which separate the types of speech associated with different roles, grammatically and lexically; the examination answer will probably keep closer to the lexical collocates of the question, a conversation answer may diverge at some points. The conversation will probably have simpler, looser sentences, more pronominal references and so on.

Formality has not a lot of relevance to answering, except that in so far as the questioner is initiator the answerer is expected to fall into line with the style of the question. Joos (1962) has suggested a five-point scale for judging formality, viz. frozen, formal, consultative, casual, intimate, and he has optimistically guessed that all natural languages have these five styles. However, as Ervin-Tripp writes (1964), this is testable only if his division of types is not arbitrary, although it is worth noting that Labov (1966) has applied Joos's separation to social-class differences in pronunciation switches, with impressive success.

We refer to Halliday's 'mode' as *medium* because 'mode' has a special connotation in this monograph, and we could think of no better word to refer to what we have in mind. Where low feedback media are used, the ideal answerer will have to take into account all the possible intentions and expectations of the questioner and provide an answer which makes allowance for this. Where he is not sure how specific his information is required to be, he will perhaps grade it in some way. In general, where the answerer is not in a position to check the reception of his answer by asking, for example, 'Does that satisfy you?' greater redundancy will be necessary in answers to questions which are at all ambiguous, e.g. where people have written an ambiguous question to some B.B.C. programme, the expert panellist may well treat the several possibilities by using conditionals, viz. 'If Mr Smith means . . . then I would say . . . but if on the other hand he means . . . then . . .' Use of speech rather than writing generally means a use of less complex structures and a looser style, since the time given for encoding is usually shorter.

Such are the constraints of register upon an answerer. How these may be differentially perceived and maintained or disregarded is the subject for later discussion (p. 72). A given register is a function of interactions across the four scales, so that one might have a 'written, non-technical, casual, narrative', for instance, or 'broadcast, formal, philosophical discussion', and so on.

Our main concern with this area of context is to *control for it*, partly out of a proper deference to the requirements of experimental design, partly because we have a particular interest in the educational confrontation of teacher and child and partly because the separations made by linguists are given only definitions and examples with no attempt at an exhaustive taxonomy. This means that in the studies we have carried out we aimed to specify the nature of the relevant features of the questioning situation, to maintain the same conditions for all experimental subjects, and to understand something of the limitations of the data obtained under such conditions. A description of some of the relevant situational features of the questions asked in the interview with five-year-old children described in Chapter 5 would look like the following. These are given as it would be from the point of view of the answerer, so that we do not include answerer characteristics in this list.

Participant features:

The questioner   The questioner was adult, female, young and middle-class. She was a stranger to the child, and hence he had no information about her

	individual knowledge, attitudes and orientations.
Other features of the immediate situation	The interviewer and child were alone together, generally in the corner of a spare classroom. The interview took place during the school day when the child would otherwise have been engaged in class activity. He was taken out of the classroom when his turn came 'to play games with Miss X'.

Register features:

(*a*) Field	We can describe the questions asked in terms of their subject-matter: (1) Specification of an invented title for a detailed picture which the children had already described. (2) Description of how to play 'Hide and Seek'. (3) Description and explanation of the workings of a mechanical toy elephant which the children had already played with and could look at.
(*b*) Role	The children were told that they were going to play games which required them to give speech when requested. For the question about the picture they were invited to answer, 'What shall we call it? For the questions about the workings of the elephant, the interviewer was blindfolded so that the child could see and examine the elephant, but the interviewer could not. This meant that if the child pointed at something rather than named it, he did not 'communicate' to the interviewer. For the question about 'Hide and Seek', the interviewer said she did not know how to play it. The child was to tell her how to play the game.
(*c*) Formality	The situation was relatively informal. The interviewer had spent a session in the children's classroom, and there were attempts to establish rapport with the child both before the interview by talking about something he had made or drawn at school,

and during the interview by being friendly and receptive to what the child said. The interview was, however, structured so that as far as possible no extra speech was introduced other than that prescribed by the schedule.

(d) Medium   The situation was face-to-face and oral. An attempt was made to keep feedback from the questioning interviewer unrelated to the content of the answer. There was no discussion of the children's answers.

While we hope that the contextual features mentioned were maintained for all children, there are other contextual features which are of interest because they point to variation between children. These are the aspects of appropriateness, completeness, and presupposition in the children's answers.

(b) APPROPRIATENESS, COMPLETENESS AND PRESUPPOSITION

(1) *Contextual appropriateness*   This is reserved for judgments about the accuracy of information given. An answer which was entirely appropriate contextually would contain no untrue information about whatever thesis it referred to, e.g. object, event, process, action, etc.

> *Example:*   Q. When will John arrive?
> A. John will arrive at four o'clock.

(i) The core of the answer is located in the adverbial group representing time. If the person referred to, viz. one John, eventually did arrive at the place referred to at four o'clock, then the answer contains no contextually inappropriate elements in the core area.

(ii) The concordant area is not generally relevant to contextual appropriateness. It only applies if a statement that is made could be untrue *because the structures of the question which are repeated or presupposed in the answer* do not supply accurate information at the time the answer is given.

> *Example:*   Q. When will John arrive?
> A. John will arrive at four o'clock.

As long as the time when the answer is given is prior to the particular four o'clock indicated then maintenance of the same tense is contextually appropriate.

(iii) The residual area is concerned with the accuracy of added information which is not germane to the concern of the question.

Example: Q. When will John arrive?
A. John will arrive at four o'clock and will bring his haversack.

If it transpires that John does arrive at four o'clock with his haversack, then the answer contains no contextually inappropriate element in the residual area, i.e. the area concerned with the added information about the presence of 'his haversack'.

(2) *Contextual completeness* This is a quantitative assessment. How much information is given, compared with how much could be given?
(i) In the core area, this aspect is only relevant to questions where there is freedom about the amount of information that can be presented.

Example: Q. Who came to dinner?
A. John Smith, Jill Smith, Fred, Albert and Josie Smith.

This would be a more complete answer, given that it was also true, than a simple mention of John Smith, but not so complete as if another person who also came to dinner, e.g. Elsie Smith, were also mentioned.
(ii) The concordant area is of minor significance here and is not always applicable.

Example: Q. Who came to dinner?
A. John Smith, Jill Smith, Fred, Albert and Josie Smith came.

If the particular intonation makes it ambiguous as to whether they came *to dinner* then we might say that this was contextually incomplete in the concordant area.
(iii) In the residual area we find it is not so much a matter of completeness or incompleteness, but of *over-completeness*, which is scored when unasked-for information is given.

Example: Q. Who came to dinner?
A. John Smith and Jill Smith, and they both wore red hats.

The information about their wearing red hats is extra, making for over-completeness in the residual area, even though the answer may be more or less incomplete in the *core* area. The extra information may or may not be true. The example given above for contextual appropriateness in the residual area could be used here.

Example: Q. When will John arrive?
A. John will arrive at four o'clock and will bring his haversack.

Thus it can be seen that the residual area is concerned with unasked-for information. Contextual appropriateness is concerned with the truth of such information. Contextual completeness with its presence and quantification.

(3) *Contextual presupposition* This concerns the answerer's apparent assumptions about the questioner's state of knowledge and other demands of the situation. Such assumptions might lead the answerer to pose his answer at a certain level of generality.

Example: Q. Who came to dinner?
A. The Smith family.

There is an apparent assumption, either that the questioner is aware of who comprise the Smith family, viz. John, Jill, Albert, Fred, etc., or that a detailed list of names is not required. An answer like the above presents a problem for the assessment of contextual completeness in the core area, i.e. whether to judge the collective term to be as complete as the detailed identification of each individual item.

Again, contextual presupposition may be manifested in the degree of lexical completeness.

Example: Q. Which sweet would you like?
A. That one.

The answer assumes a situation where an ostensive expression, possibly accompanied by pointing, is a sufficient clue to separate out the intended sweet.

The mode of answer may also reveal certain assumptions.

Example: Q. Where did you leave your umbrella?
A. By the long bench. (Mode 3 for 'where' questions. See p. 58).

The answerer assumes that 'the long bench' is known to the questioner.

All answers make certain fundamental presuppositions—for instance, that the answer is being received, that it will be understood and so on. What we are particularly interested in is the possibility of answers containing invalid assumptions. Our first definition of presupposition (p. 25) limited it to the failure to supply something because it was already given. As far as contextual presupposition is concerned, what is supplied or not is in the form of information. Where information of a certain amount or type is not supplied, apparently because it was assumed to be known already and yet was not, there is invalid presupposition. Where the information not given is correctly assumed to be known already, then there is still presupposition, but it is valid. In some cases redundant information may be given *in case* it is not known already. We do not treat this as invalid, but as a failure to presuppose.

The category of contextual presupposition has not as yet been systematically applied to empirical data, although Flavell and his co-workers (1968) have performed a series of experiments illustrating developmental changes in children, Schatzman and Strauss (1955) have demonstrated dramatic social-class differences in descriptions of a local earthquake, and a major aspect of Bernstein's thinking emphasizes that lower-working-class speech, while making valid assumptions in conversation with friends, fails to adapt when confronted with strangers. It still awaits sufficient refinement of conception to enable it to be operationalized. We shall none the less refer to it in a discussion of the results obtained in the other categories, e.g. mode of answer, lexical incompleteness, contextual completeness, etc., for it is from the examination of these other categories that we hope to discover what sort of place contextual presupposition might have in a scheme for the analysis of answers.

(xi) Mode

We have already mentioned how a question may be open to various interpretations, according to differing amounts and types of information demanded along with their grammatical and lexical correlates.

Where there are distinguishable and specifiable ways of interpreting a question type (defined by its interrogative group, e.g. a 'why' question, a 'where from' question, etc.) which are related to distinct specifiable ways of giving answers according to different 'points of view', these ways are called *modes* of answer. We do not claim to have separated all possible modes for all types of question. Our selections, at this stage at least, are somewhat arbitrary. They are governed by (1) what seem to us to be obviously separable ways of answering, and (2) the expectation that certain known psychological and social variables will lead to differential ways of answering according to different 'points of view'. In a given instance, there may be contextual reasons which predispose towards the use of one mode rather than another, and frequently linguistic markers separate modes from one another. Hence, when judgments are made about the mode of answer selected, context should be taken into account, and when judgments are made about its form, mode will be relevant. Separate modes of answer are applicable to intra-question mode choices, so that a 'how' mode 3 question offers different answer modes according to manner and process (see p. 60). Different empirical situations may continue to show up new modes of answering for the various question types. In any given analysis of answering behaviour modes may be subcategorized according to further areas of interest.

> *Example:* Q. Why shouldn't anyone steal?
> A.1. Because they get found out and punished.
> A.2. Because the people will miss their belongings.

We consider that both of these answers are appeals to consequence, which is a mode. They may be further subcategorized according to whether they are oriented towards: (1) the *actor*, in this case the subject of the question, viz. 'anyone', or (2) some *other*. These subcategorizations within mode are related to the specific type of content in the question. Here the content is concerned with a moral justification.

An example showing how a question allows answering across a range of modes will probably help to clarify the idea of mode. 'Where' questions appear to offer three modes of answer.

> *Example:* Q. Where is the Post Office?
> A.1. In Stanley Street.
> A.2. Two hundred yards from here.
> A.3. Next to 'The George and Dragon'.

We call these modes (1) absolute place, (2) place relative to present location, (3) place relative to some other named point. Mode 1 is not in fact absolute, but is a more objective indication than the other two, and perhaps modes 1 and 3 should be regarded as approximating to the opposite ends of a continuum of objectivity, while mode 2 always relates to the present place.

(1) *Appropriateness of mode* There has been no systematic categorization of modes as appropriate or inappropriate. It is hoped that the basis for such a categorization will emerge as we apply the modes to empirical data and find out just how they are used.

It may be that some modes will be more acceptable in the majority of cases than others. One of our modes for 'why' questions, 'restatement of the question as an answer' might qualify in practically all cases as an inappropriate mode, since it offers no new content apart from that which was in the question. Often the context in which the question-answer event occurs will make one mode more acceptable than another.

> *Example:* Q. How do I get to the police station?
> A.1. By bus.
> A.2. You turn right at the end of the road, then take the second road to the left and you will find it halfway down on the left.

The example demonstrates two answer modes for a mode 3 'how' question—namely, A.1 method and A.2 process. If the questioner is aware of the location of the police station and is wondering what method of transport is available for him, then valid contextual presupposition on the part of the answerer would mean that the answer should contain the first mode. But if the questioner has stopped someone in the street and asked them the above question, then it might be normal to assume that the second mode is more acceptable.

Modes may also be judged more or less appropriate according to the content of the question.

> *Example:* Q. Why does it get dark at night?
> A.1. Because the earth spins round on its axis, . . .
> A.2. So that it is light on the other side of the world and . . .

It might be that the investiture of such specific functions (A.2) in a natural phenomenon would be considered an inappropriate use of the mode 'consequence' while mention of causal factors (A.1) would not. This is a separate consideration from that involving contextual presupposition about the intention of the questioner, i.e. what sort of mode of answer he is expecting to receive.

(2) *Completeness of mode* The measure of this consists simply of a count of the number of different modes used—the range of modes for any given answer.

> *Example:* Q. When did you come back from America?
> A.1. The year before last, 1966.
> A.2. When I was eighty-four.

A.1. contains two modes, viz. 'time from present' and 'absolute' time, A.2 only one, viz. 'time relative to the age of the actor' (p. 59).

D

Thus the first answer is more complete with regard to mode than the second.

(3) *Presupposition of mode*   There is as yet no conception of a separate area called 'presupposition of mode'. Contextual reasons for giving one mode rather than another are dealt with under 'contextual presupposition' and evaluated under 'appropriateness of mode 'and' the measure of range', i.e. how many and which modes are given under 'completeness of mode'. We shall, nevertheless, keep the category, since the application of the three aspects within mode is at present rather unstable, and a refinement of our scheme might delegate some of the areas at present covered by appropriateness and completeness of mode to this category of presupposition. The refinement of the category 'contextual presupposition' should help to elucidate a possible function for this.

(xii) Form

Form is the linguistic level at which categories are applied to linguistic substance, whether this substance is *phonic*, consisting of vocal sounds, or *graphic*, consisting of written marks.

Within form we have a separation between *grammar* and *lexis* (described as two demi-levels). Grammar has been defined as 'that part of the study of language which deals with forms and the structure of words (MORPHOLOGY) and with their customary arrangements in phrases and sentences (SYNTAX)' (Pei, 1966). It is basically concerned with rules governing (1) the selection of items from paradigms offering a limited set of possibilities, and (2) the combination of such selected items into larger wholes (syntagmes). The particular grammatical description which we shall be using is based upon Halliday's Scale and Category Grammar (Halliday *et al.*, 1964). A limited knowledge of the grammar will be assumed in the subsequent description of the formal analysis of answers, but it is hoped that the examples we supply will be sufficiently illustrative of the points we wish to make, to compensate for any lack of information about this grammar on the part of the reader. Whereas grammar is concerned with the selection of an item from a limited set, lexis involves selection from a much wider set. This may be illustrated within the verbal group:

Example: The boy was hit.

If we assume one interpretation of the meaning of this sentence, the verbal group is 'was hit'. The *grammatical* systemic choices involved in the choice of this verb form include: one within number, where the singular rather than the plural form is selected; one within voice, where the passive rather than active is selected; one within tense, where the simple past perfect is selected. The *lexical* choice involves the selection of 'to hit' rather than 'to miss', 'to thrash', 'to love', 'to shock', and so on through the total list of transitive verbs.

According to Sinclair (1966) a lexical item is 'a formal item (at least one morpheme long) whose pattern of occurrence can be described in terms of a uniquely ordered series of other lexical items occurring in its environment' (p. 412).

The study of lexis is then a statistical study. A theory of lexis might be said to contain two categories: (1) collocation, and (2) lexical set (Dixon, 1963). Sinclair and Dixon appear to differ over what is to be meant by 'lexical set'. For Sinclair it is something which 'parallels the categories of a thesaurus', a distinct group of frequently associating collocates which presumably could be given a single grouping label (*op. cit.*, p. 427). For Dixon a lexical set consists of those items related together in such a way that they can occur in very similar linguistic environments—near-synonyms, in fact. Collocation seeks to specify the probability for a given lexical item of other items occurring next to it or next but one to it and so on, or else within a certain 'span' of items on either side of a given 'nodal' item.

When specifying our formal criteria for judging whether a given response should be called an answer, we included lexical continuity. We are not interested in obtaining exact probabilities of given items occurring, but with assessing the relevance of the response to the question asked.

Example: Q. Why do the leaves fall off the trees?
    A.1. The bag is standing by the door.
    A.2. The hedgehog hibernates in winter.
    A.3. The sap goes down and the leaves shrivel and die.

A.1 seems to have no lexical continuity with the question. A.2 is marginal, since the two events might be linked by the item 'winter', which collocates with the 'leaves falling off trees'. The third answer, A.3, has obvious continuity, both in terms of collocation and through the repetition of the item 'leaves'.

When we apply our categories of appropriateness, completeness and presupposition to answers, we seek to judge the selection of lexical items in terms of what could have been selected in their place to give a meaningful, accurate, precise answer. In doing this we make use of contextual criteria in so far as the relationship of correspondence between words and things prescribes limits on lexical choices.

As we proceed to describe our scheme for the formal analysis of answers, we shall pick up again the three areas of answer relevant

to appropriateness and completeness, viz. the core area, the concordant area, and the residual area.

(a) FORMAL APPROPRIATENESS: GRAMMATICAL

(i) Within the core area: frequently a particular grammatical class
of item is required by the question to be given in the answer.

> *Example:* Q. Where did you go to school?
> A.1. In Exton.
> A.2. On Tuesday.

The question requires either that there be an adverbial group or that
there be an 'adverbial' clause, e.g. 'Where the bee sucks'. Both A.1
and A.2 fulfil that requirement. However, whereas the first answer
fulfils a further requirement, viz. that such a group should represent
'place', the second does not and is therefore inappropriate.

Often, as in the above example, the required grammatical item
can be called a *replacement group* for the interrogative group, since
it is possible for the interrogative group to be taken out and the
replacement group substituted in the sentence frame of the question
(after transformation to the declarative) in order to obtain an answer
statement. For the above example, A.1, this statement would be:
'I went to school in Exton.'

A replacement group is not a necessary feature for answers to all
types of questions. Where a process is recounted in response to a
mode 3 'how' question, this may not contain an adverbial group of
manner, and an answer to a 'why' question does not have to contain a
'because' or a 'so that' type of conditioning clause. However, such
types and modes do allow the possibility of answering with a
definable replacement group, and there is also the negative restric-
tion against using a replacement group belonging to another question
type as a 'core' feature of the answer.

> *Example:* Q. Why did you leave the country?
> A. By plane

The answer to this 'why' question consists of a replacement group
for a 'how' question. It is therefore inappropriate in the 'core' area.
(ii) Within the concordant area: the systemic choices in the question
are required to be maintained in the answer. Such choices include
tense, number, person, case, gender, etc. We have decided that this
sort of requirement should be interpreted at the 'deep' level for
certain cases. Where polarity is concerned for instance, normally a
repeated verb should be in the same polarity.

Example: Q. Where did you go to school?
     A.1. Not in Exton.
     A.2. I did not go to school in Exton.
     A.3. I did not go to school anywhere else but in Exton.

The first two answers, A.1 and A.2, fail to maintain the same polarity in any sense and are therefore inappropriate. The third, A.3, however resolves itself by a sort of double-negative construction, and thus maintains the same polarity as the question at the deep level. Similarly, it is required that the actor, action, goal relations of the question are maintained rather than the active and passive voice of the verb.

Example: Q. Who was hit by John?
     A.1. John hit me.
     A.2. John was hit by me.

The first answer, A.1, maintains the same actor, viz. John, although the voice in the answer is different from that in the question. This is appropriate. In the second answer, John is no longer actor, although the passive tense is preserved. This is inappropriate.

An exception to the polarity requirement above occurs when a question indicates a dimension by specifying one end (as the unmarked term).

Example: Q. How tall are you?
     A.1. Not very.
     A.2. Quite short.

Answers A.1 and A.2 are both judged appropriate, since the question was asking for the specification of a place in the total tall-short continuum rather than just the 'tall' half of it.

(iii) Within the residual area: the breaking of any grammatical rules in the answer which either are not criterial for its evaluation as an appropriate answer to a particular question type, or are not those governing concord between question and answer, makes for inappropriateness. In other words, the answer is looked at in isolation as a word, group, clause, sentence or set of sentences in its own right and then 'judged' for such grammatical faults as intra-answer discord, incompatible juxtapositions of parts of speech, misorderings, etc.

Example: Q. Where did you go to school?
     A. I wented to school down Exton.

The above answer contains two instances of inappropriateness in the residual area. The past tense of 'to go' does not require the addition of the morpheme 'ed'. The requirements of the core area do not go beyond specifying an adverbial group of place, and these are fulfilled in the above example. However, it is thought that the name of a town, 'Exton', cannot acceptably act as complement to the preposition 'down'. We are aware that in making such judgments as this we lay ourselves open to the charge of confusing dialect differences with variations in grammaticality. This instance is a marginal decision which well illustrates the ambiguity.

(b) FORMAL APPROPRIATENESS: LEXICAL

(i) Within the core area: lexical items occurring in the replacement group are to be informative and not mere repetitions of items in the question.

> *Example:* Q. Where did you go to school?
> A.1. In school.
> A.2. Where the teachers were.

Both answers A.1 and A.2 are *grammatically* appropriate in the core area. However, they are both *lexically* inappropriate, since the first simply repeats 'school' from the question and does not answer *where* the school was, and the second gives no information if we consider that the presence of teachers is part of the definition of school.

(ii) Within the concordant area: at least part of the structure of the question is repeated in the answer. To be appropriate the relation between the lexical items contained in the structure and what they refer to must be maintained.

> *Example:* Q. Where did you go to school?
> A.1 Jim went to school in Exton.
> A.2 I was educated in Exton.

The first answer is lexically inappropriate if the 'you' of the question is singular and does not refer to 'Jim'. The substitution of a synonymous expression for 'going to school', viz. 'being educated', is not, however, considered inappropriate. It may sometimes be difficult to draw the line between those near-synonym substitutions which are appropriate and those which are not.

(iii) Within the residual area: we are interested in the appropriate use of lexical items for making particular references. It is sometimes obvious that a person means something other than what they say.

Example: Q. Where did you go to school?
A. In Exbury.

In the above example, the answer demonstrates the third type of lexical inappropriateness, if the intention was to refer to Exton and not to a place called 'Exbury'. In some cases this phenomenon will be very difficult to distinguish from contextual inappropriateness; in others the linguistic or situation context will reveal it.

(c) FORMAL COMPLETENESS: GRAMMATICAL

(i) Within the core area: to qualify as grammatically complete, the whole of the structure of a required replacement group must be there, so that the answer does not look more like one to a different question type.

Example: Q. Where did you go to school?
A. The same place as my sister.

If it were regarded as complete in its present form, the answer in the above example would be better interpreted as the answer to such a question as 'Which was the place where you went to school?' which demands a nominal group, such as that given in the example. We could treat such an answer as grammatically inappropriate rather than grammatically incomplete and argue that it required a preposition like 'at' or 'in', since we have no proof that the above answer functions as an adverbial group for the answerer, or that he recognizes the difference between the two question types. It was thought that such an answer bears a closer resemblance to other types of grammatical incompleteness than it does to grammatical inappropriateness, but subsequent empirical investigations may show that this intuition is invalid.

(ii) Within the concordant area: all grammatical presupposition could be equated with grammatical incompleteness, but we have decided to separate out those instances where grammatical presupposition is imperfectly carried out.

Example: Q. Where did you go in the car?
A.1 To London.
A.2 I went to London in the car.
A.3 I went to London in.

A.1 is the case of complete maximal presupposition, A.2 of complete minimal presupposition. A.3 presupposes 'the car' in an unacceptable way, producing an uncompleted group which is part of a clause containing other completed groups. It is also doubtful whether an answer like:

A.4. To London in the car.

is an acceptable form of presupposition rather than an incomplete version of minimal grammatical presupposition.

(iii) Within the residual area: grammatical incompleteness is scored for any omission of a necessary element of structure which (*a*) does not make the answer look like one to a different question type (i), and (*b*) is not presupposed in the question (ii). Such an omission may be of a free clause from a sentence, a preposition from an adverbial group requiring one, a nominal group head or (more often) a modifier, and so on.

> *Example:* Q. How do you ride a bicycle?
> A. You sit on the saddle, put your feet . . . the pedals.
> When you pedal . . . bike, . . .

The omission marks in the example answer above point to three instances of incompleteness, the first being the omission of a preposition from the adverbial group ' . . . the pedals' the second of a deictic modifier in the nominal group ' . . . bike', the third of a free clause in the sentence containing the bound clause, 'when you pedal . . . bike, . . . '

(*d*) FORMAL COMPLETENESS: LEXICAL

(i) Within the core area: lexical completeness demands that where there is a replacement group (p. 40) the lexical items which realize this should not be what we might call 'vague markers'. Also we might stipulate that where there is no replacement group, those lexical items which mark the relationship of the answer to the particular question posed should not be 'vague markers'.

> *Example:* Q. Where did you go to school?
> A.1. Near the thing.
> A.2. Over there.

In the above example, 'thing' substitutes for a more explicit reference, so A.1 may be called lexically incomplete. It was originally decided that lexical incompleteness should be assessed by reference to context, so that A.2 accompanied by pointing to the relevant place would be called lexically complete because of valid contextual presupposition. This decision was reversed, so that we make judgments about lexis independently from judgments about context, as these levels are separated in this scheme. This means that a lexically incomplete answer or one containing lexically incomplete elements may in the context be every bit as adequate as a lexically complete answer. Conversely, an answer which is lexically complete may be relatively incomplete contextually, failing to supply all the information which the questioner would find relevant.

(ii) Within the concordant area: we do not recognize a separate possibility for lexical completeness. We could (just as was suggested for grammatical completeness) regard it as the other side of the coin of presupposition, so that the greater the presupposition the less complete the answer, but we do not do this. Neither do we find it feasible to look for incomplete lexical presupposition, since this does not seem to occur.

(iii) Within the residual area: vagueness, imprecision and the use of pronouns without having made prior reference with nouns, all count as lexical incompleteness. In fact, these are the same sort of 'vague markers' as for (i) above, but which do not occur either in the replacement group or as one of the key lexical items for answers without replacement groups. Also included here are vague expressions which are added to the answer, but provide no information, except perhaps to signal in an indirect way that the answerer is unsure about the value of the answer or that there is more to be said about any one of a number of things, but which will not be said by him now.

> *Example:* Q. Where did you go to school?
> A. In Exton, sort of thing.

The crucial information is given, viz. 'In Exton', that will satisfy the formal requirements of the core area. 'Sort of thing' is added.

(e) FORMAL PRESUPPOSITION: GRAMMATICAL

Presupposition of elements in the question is only possible for answers containing a replacement group. Maximal grammatical presupposition occurs when the replacement group is at the lowest possible rank and is given alone.

> *Example:* Q. Where does the water in the tap come from?
> A.1. The reservoir.
> A.2. From the reservoir.

In the above example, A.1 manifests maximal presupposition. It is the shortest answer that is possible within the limitations of grammatical completeness. It constitutes a replacement group for 'where from'. The answer A.2 only replaces the 'where', and thus provides an intermediate degree of presupposition. An answer making minimal grammatical presupposition, which in fact is none at all, would be as follows:

> A.3. The water in the tap comes from the reservoir.

A new sentence is supplied as the answer which does not depend for its structural completeness on any elements of the question. It is always possible to give an answer containing no presupposition, and generally it is possible to make maximal presupposition, even though this might not be stylistically appropriate to the content of the information. Intermediate degrees of presupposition are not always available.

> *Example:* Q. Why did he come?
> A.1. He came because he was called.
> A.2. He was called.
> A.3. Because he was called.

These three answers give two instances (1 and 2) of minimal presupposition and one (3) of maximal presupposition. There is no possibility for anything in between. Although A.2 does not give any more information than A.3, it is reckoned complete and non-presuppositive, both because it is a free clause and can stand alone acceptably and, more importantly, because it cannot be fitted back into the question in place of the previous adjunct exponent, 'why', which is the criterion for a replacement group. It would be possible to regard A.2 as 'containing' an elided 'because', but we have decided that this would be an unnecessary complication. If we did not consider that a special grammatical relationship existed between questions and answers, an answer like 'The reservoir' to 'Where does the water in the tap come from?' would be considered in isolation from the question as (in Scale and Category terms) a sentence, consisting of one free clause, consisting of one nominal group, consisting of two words. It was the notion of the replacement group, which in the first place led us to consider presuppositive answers incomplete, though in an acceptable way. We regard them as sentences requiring elements from the interrogatively formed preceding question for their completion.

There is a problem about how we should regard answers beginning with 'It is', which may either be anaphoric references back to part of a question or kataphoric references forward to something yet to be mentioned *or presupposed*.

> *Example:* Q. Why do the leaves fall off the trees?
> A. It is because they die.

The above answerer may be using 'it is' to refer back to 'the leaves fall off the trees', or else he may be using the theme-predication device for stressing the bound clause, 'because they die', presupposing '(that) the leaves fall off the trees' after the bound clause.

If the former is taken to be the case, then we might say that the answer is, grammatically, minimally presuppositive and that a rather exceptional use of lexical presupposition is involved. ('It' normally substitutes for a noun in lexical presupposition rather than for a clause, as could be the case here.) If the latter is assumed, we might call it maximal presupposition with an added device for stress. A compromise has placed such an answer under 'intermediate' presupposition by taking the number of units (here counted by clause) as the criterial attribute.

(f) FORMAL PRESUPPOSITION: LEXICAL

Lexical presupposition involves any one of a variety of substitutions in the answer for elements in the question: pronouns for nouns, general-purpose verbs like 'get', 'go' and especially 'do' for verbs, words like 'here' and 'then' for more precise place- and time-markers.

Example: Q. Who drove to London with Jim last Tuesday?
              A. Jane went there with him then.

Another possible candidate for lexical presupposition has already been noted, viz. when 'It + to be' occurs at the beginning of an answer. Sometimes also this presupposition is not of single elements.

Example: Q. Who is playing the piano?
              A. John is doing it.

In this case lexical presupposition yields 'is doing it' in place of 'is playing the piano'. The construction 'do it' can substitute for a range of structures from whole predicates to intransitive verbs, and we do not treat 'do' as a substitute for 'play' nor 'it' for 'the piano'.

Lexical presupposition is inevitably associated with the concordant area, but this does not mean that items of lexical presupposition must never be located within the grammatically defined core area.

Example: Q. Why do the leaves fall off the trees?
              A. Because they grow old and die.

'They' in the answer lexically presupposes 'leaves' in the question. It occurs within the structure of the grammatical core, but is a feature of the concordant area.

FIG. 2.1 *Application of aspects of answers to levels of analysis*

	Aspect of answer		
Level of analysis	*Appropriateness*	*Completeness*	*Presupposition*
Context	CORE Concordant <u>Residual</u>	<u>Core</u> Concordant RESIDUAL	?
Mode	CORE concordant residual	<u>Core</u> concordant residual	?
Form Grammar	CORE CONCORDANT RESIDUAL	<u>Core</u> Concordant <u>Residual</u>	Not applicable to separate areas
Form Lexis	CORE* CONCORDANT RESIDUAL	CORE* concordant RESIDUAL	core <u>Concordant</u> residual

* In these two cases the applicability is contingent upon the presence of grammatically appropriate core items.

Key: **CAPS.** means 'always applicable'.
CAP. first letter, plus underlining means 'sometimes applicable'.
Small letter means 'never applicable'.

Chapter 3 Aspects of answers: the analysis system in application

It may help to clarify the ideas put forward in Chapter 2 if we look at the different interrogatives separately and note the particular prominent features of each as they are related to the proposed scheme of analysis.

A 'who' question is used as an example to which we apply the categories mentioned in Chapter 2. The other interrogatives are dealt with only in so far as they differ from 'who' or from one another.

(*1*) *An example for 'who' questions*
   (i) Mode
  (ii) Form:
      (*a*) Inappropriateness: grammatical
                                  lexical
      (*b*) Incompleteness: grammatical
                                    lexical
      (*c*) Presupposition: grammatical
                                    lexical
 (iii) Context:
      (*a*) Inappropriateness
      (*b*) Incompleteness and over-completeness
      (*c*) Presupposition
(*2*) *Where*
(*3*) *When*
(*4*) *How*
(*5*) *Why*
(*6*) *Which and what*
      (*i*) Which
     (*ii*) What

1 An example for 'who' questions

The sample question to be considered is: 'Who are standing over there?' We discuss the possible types of variation in answering under the headings of Mode, Form and Content, the latter two levels being associated with the three aspects of appropriateness, completeness and presupposition. It is not thought necessary to give detailed examples of various forms of appropriateness, completeness and presupposition for 'Modes of Answer'. 'Who' questions at present offer only two modes of answer.

(i) Mode of answer

It will be remembered that we consider 'who' to function within the referential category Identification, subset Persons, and we have at present separated two modes of person identification which we could call (1) Unique Person Specification, and (2) Role Specification. Which mode is selected may depend upon situational factors. If asked 'Who are standing there?' under some circumstances, the questioner is more likely to be satisfied with 'The Imperial Bodyguard' than a Widdicombe Fair list of their names. For particular occasions, the questioner will often find it more useful to learn that the milkman rather than Mr Jones is at the door. In certain instances the two may be combined, as, for example, 'Dr. Smith'.

(ii) Form of answer

The criterion of replaceability applies: to give a formally appropriate and complete answer to the question with no presupposition, there should be a transformation of the question from the interrogative to the declarative form, while 'who' should be replaced by a nominal group which makes precise informative reference to the uniquely relevant person or persons referred to in the question.

Basic Example Question: Who are standing there?
Linguistic Structure: Shw Pt08 Av6*

Answers of maximal appropriateness and completeness and minimal presupposition:

Mode (1) John and Jill Smith are standing there.
Mode (2) The butler and the chambermaid are standing there.

The types of deviation from the requirements of grammatical and lexical appropriateness, completeness and various possibilities for presupposition are discussed under the headings, Inappropriateness, Incompleteness, and Presupposition. For inappropriateness and incompleteness, deviations in the secondary separation into (i) core,

* This notational system is described at length by Turner and Mohan (1970). It is included for interested linguists, but a knowledge of the system is not necessary for an understanding of the text.

(ii) concordant and (iii) residual sentence areas of the answer are described and exemplified.

(a) *FORMAL INAPPROPRIATENESS: GRAMMATICAL*

(i) Core: Grammatical inappropriateness is any substitution for John Smith which is not a nominal group head.

> e.g. *Because it is not crowded.*

(ii) Concordant: Discordance occurs as a result of a shift in tense, person, number or gender relative to that used in the question.

> e.g. Jill Smith and John Smith *were* standing there.

(iii) Residual: A grammatical mistake may be present which consists neither of a failure to meet the requirements of the interrogative nor a failure to maintain concord with the question.

> e.g. Jill Smith and John Smith are standing there by *them* gates.
> or Jill Smith and John Smith *is* standing there.

In the second answer the discord is taken to be within the answer rather than between the question and answer.

(b) *FORMAL INAPPROPRIATENESS: LEXICAL*

(i) Core: Lexical inappropriateness consists of any substitution for John Smith which:

(*a*) is a nominal group head but does not refer to a person, or
(*b*) is so uninformative that the answer could have been deduced from the question.

> e.g. (*a*) The *umbrellas* are standing there.
> (*b*) *People* are standing there. ('Who' necessarily refers to people.)

(ii) Concordant: Discordant lexis results from a significant change of wording.

> e.g. John Smith and Jill Smith are *sitting* there.

(iii) Residual: The third type of lexical inappropriateness consists of, for example, the use of a malapropism in any addition to the question's content or a mistake in naming someone in the replacement group.

> e.g. John Smith and Jill Smith are standing there by the *emolument.*
> *Jim* Smith and Jill Smith are standing there.

(c) FORMAL INCOMPLETENESS: GRAMMATICAL

(i) Core: Grammatical incompleteness results from the omission of some element of structure in the answer which appears to render it a more appropriate answer to a *different* question. Since replacement groups for 'who' are nominal, except where they consist of rank-shifted clauses, and cannot contain groups which are other than nominal, grammatical incompleteness does not apply in area (i) for 'who' questions.

(ii) Concordant: Incompleteness results from an omission of a grammatical element contained in the question.

e.g. John Smith and Jill Smith . . . standing there.

(iii) Residual: The omission of an element not contained in the question or demanded for an appropriate answer in the core area counts as grammatically incomplete.

e.g. John Smith . . . Jill Smith are standing there.

(d) FORMAL INCOMPLETENESS: LEXICAL

(i) Core: To count as lexically incomplete, the essential part of the answer must be expounded by a general, vague lexical item rather than one giving specific identification.

e.g. *A couple* are standing there.

(ii) Concordant: The substitution for lexical items in the question of more general expressions is dealt with under lexical presupposition. There is no category of lexical incompleteness in the concordant area.

(iii) Residual: Lexical incompleteness is achieved by the use of a vague expression either (*a*) in the place of something which would be more explicit somewhere other than in the core or, (*b*) as an addition which adds no information.

e.g. (*a*) John Smith and Jill Smith are standing there by the *thing*.
(*b*) John Smith and Jill Smith are *sort of like* standing there.

(e) FORMAL PRESUPPOSITION: GRAMMATICAL

Grammatical presupposition involves the omission of certain linguistic structures in an answer because these are taken as understood in that they were given in the question. Grammatical presupposition necessarily involves the whole answer, so that it is not possible to look for it *within* answer areas. There is a relationship, however, between grammatical presupposition and answer areas; it is through making what we call maximal grammatical presupposition that we can discover the essential core area of the answer if this is a replacement group, since that is what remains. Answers to our sample question are presented as they fall under the three degrees of presupposition, maximal and minimal and intermediate.

1 *Maximal presupposition*

e.g. John Smith and Jill Smith

Given	*Presupposed*
Shpq + hpq	PtO8 Av6
John Smith and Jill Smith	Are standing there

2 *Minimal presupposition*

e.g. John Smith and Jill Smith are standing there

Given	*Presupposed*
Shpq + hpq PtO8 Av6	—
John Smith and Jill Smith are standing there	

3 *Intermediate presupposition*

e.g. (*a*) Jill Smith and John Smith are

Given	*Presupposed*
Shpq + hpq PtO2	PytO8 Av6
Jill and John Smith are	standing there

(*b*) It is Jill Smith and John Smith

Given	*Presupposed*
S mhpq + hpq	PaitO8 Av6
It is Jill Smith and John Smith	standing there
or Shp4 PletO2 Chpq + hpq	B^2 Shw PtO8 Av6
It is Jill Smith and John Smith	who are standing there

(*f*) *FORMAL PRESUPPOSITION: LEXICAL*

Lexical presupposition can only occur in the concordant answer area (ii), since it is specifically concerned with parallels between question and answer items. It is when a substitute form is used in the answer for a noun or verb in the question that an instance of lexical presupposition is scored.

E

e.g. Jill Smith and John Smith *are doing it.*

'Are doing it' is a substitute for the whole of the predicate 'are standing there'.

(iii) Context of answer

The same aspects of appropriateness, completeness and presupposition are relevant at the level of context.

We shall keep the same example as that used for form and mode contrasts.

Basic example: Q. Who are standing there?
A. John Smith and Jill Smith are standing there.

If the answerer has understood the meaning of the question, so that, for example, he is referring to the same place (there) as that referred to by the questioner and he is sufficiently aware of the questioner's state of knowledge and intentions to realize that John Smith and Jill Smith are unique identifications, then his level of presupposition is adequate. If John Smith and Jill Smith are in fact standing there and if there is nobody else standing there, then the answer is both appropriate and maximally complete.

For judgments of contextual inappropriateness and relative incompleteness we shall keep the same division into answer areas which we used for form. Since the interlevel of context links form to situation, the application of contextual categories will have to be undertaken with reference, not just to our formal linguistic material, but to relevant situational features as well. In laying out examples, we shall set down our formal material on the left-hand side of the page and the relevant situational features on the right. The relationship between the two provides the information necessary for ascribing contextual appropriateness or inappropriateness, the degree of contextual completeness, and the type and amount of presupposition.

(a) *CONTEXTUAL INAPPROPRIATENESS*

(i) Core: If any part of the required structure given does not refer to a true fact then that element may be treated as inappropriate.

e.g. Joe Brown and Bill Robinson are standing there.
No two people of those names are standing there.

e.g. John Smith and his sister Jill Smith are standing there.
Although John Smith and Jill Smith are standing there, Jill Smith is not

the sister of John Smith.
('Sister' is taken as a role
specification.)

(ii) Concordant: The only possibility for contextual inappropriateness in the area of concordance is if whatever is said is no longer
true at the time the answer is given.

| e.g. John Smith and Jill Smith are standing there. | By the time the answer is given, Jill and John Smith have sat down. |

(iii) Residual: If information additional to that presented within the
required structure is given and any part of this information is not
true, then it may be counted as a contextually inappropriate element.

| e.g. John Smith, whom I met last week, and Jill Smith are standing there. | Although John Smith and Jill Smith are standing there, the speaker did not meet that John Smith last week. |
| e.g. John Smith and Jill Smith are standing there, in front of the library. | Although John Smith and Jill Smith are standing there, the building behind them is not the library. |

(b) CONTEXTUAL INCOMPLETENESS AND OVER-COMPLETENESS

(i) Core: Judgments of contextual incompleteness are often relative,
e.g. in cases where there is a considerable amount of discretion as
to how much information can be given and answers may be compared and ranked with one another according to how many items
of information are given. For our example, however, given that
there are only two people to be specified, the sole possibility for incompleteness is the mentioning of only one.

| e.g. Jill Smith is standing there. | Jill Smith is standing there, but so also is John Smith. |

(ii) Concordant: It is possible that there are answers which might
qualify as contextually incomplete in the second answer area.

| e.g. John Smith and Jill Smith are standing. | John Smith and Jill Smith are standing and are standing *there*, although the answerer remains uncommitted on this point. |

(iii) Residual: Information conveyed in a form other than that required by the question is not strictly necessary: it may even be irrelevant and hence *overcomplete*.

e.g. John Smith and Jill Smith are standing there. They are both wearing grey coats and carrying umbrellas.

John Smith and Jill Smith are standing there. They are both wearing grey coats and carrying umbrellas. but a description of their clothes and belongings was not asked for.

(c) CONTEXTUAL PRESUPPOSITION

There are always assumptions made about how much another person knows or understands or what form he requires an answer to be presented in. We judge these assumptions from the answer which is given. A lexically incomplete answer may or may not demonstrate what might be called invalid or even inappropriate presupposition (p. 44).

e.g. It is that couple again.

This answer may be quite satisfactory for the questioner if he has had repeated experience of Jill Smith and John Smith whom he now knows as 'that couple'. If this experience is only true for the answerer, however, such presupposition is invalid.

Where contextual presupposition is inadequate for effective communication, this may be resolved by the questioner posing a new question formed with the replacement group of the answer prefaced by 'who'+verb.

e.g. Who is that couple?

Our criteria for applying the three aspects at the three levels to answers to 'who' questions may be summarized in the following way:

Criteria: Appropriateness	Conditions of meeting criteria
1 Grammar (i) Core	Nominal group at subject.
(ii) Concordant	All grammatical choices concordant with those in the question.
(iii) Residual	All other grammatical choices 'correct'.

2	Lexis	(i) Core	Nominal group which is informative referring to role specification or unique person.
		(ii) Concordant	Adequate reproduction of the words in the question.
		(iii) Residual	All other lexical choices 'correct'.
3	Context	(i) Core	The correct person specified.
		(ii) Concordant	Information repeated from the question is true at the time the answer is given.
		(iii) Residual	Any additional information correct.

Criteria: completeness			*Conditions of meeting criteria*
1	Grammar	(i) Core	All grammatical elements present to give required nominal group. (For a 'who' question there can be no grammatical incompleteness in the core.)
		(ii) Concordant	All the necessary grammatical elements repeated in the answer.
		(iii) Residual	All other grammatical structures containing all required elements.
2	Lexis	(i) Core	Specific identification is given.
		(ii) Concordant	
		(iii) Residual	No vague expressions used other than in the nominal group head or in area (ii).
3	Context	(i) Core	All relevant persons specified.
		(ii) Concordant	All the conditions of the question answered.
		(iii) Residual	No information given which was not explicitly asked for.

| *Criteria: presupposition* | *Conditions of meeting criteria* |
| 1 Grammar | If the replacement group is substituted in the unchanged original sentence frame after a declarative transformation, no presupposition has occurred. |

| 2 Lexis | If there are no verbal group or nominal group substitute words used for verbs and nouns of the question, no presupposition has occurred. |
| 3 Context | Contextual presupposition is always present. To be valid it must take into account the questioner's relevant knowledge about the persons, and his intention in asking the question. |

Where the question is of the form 'Who is that?', the word order of a complete answer is inverted and the appropriate linguistic structure becomes a nominal group as complement rather than subject. The other variants of 'who' questions, e.g. whose, to whom, by whom, because of whom, have the same properties as 'who', *mutatis mutandis*, while the appropriate grammar and lexis will be isomorphic with the 'who' of the original question.

Other forms of questions which are referentially similar to 'who' are: 'What is the name of . . . ?', 'Which (what) person . . . ?', 'What are those people?' and these separate out the acceptable modes of answer with greater precision, the first demanding a proper name and the last a role specification.

2 Where

A 'where' question demands that information be given which locates an event or object in space. The possible structures which serve this function are adverbial groups of place expounded by lexical items specifying a particular location or by conditioning clauses containing 'where' or some other marker of space.

We have separated three modes of answer to 'where' questions: (1) map references and common knowledge; (2) place relative to present location; (3) place relative to mutually shared knowledge of a private sort. (1) could be restricted to map references alone, i.e. longitude, latitude, and grid reference, but it seems more sensible to allow 'reasonable' shared knowledge, e.g. 'In London'. This makes the distinction between (1) and (3) relative rather than absolute, but (3) will generally refer to remarks like 'near my home', where the questioner is assumed to be aware of where my home is.

Example: Q. Where does John Smith live?
   A. Mode (1) In Berkeley Street, London.
   A. Mode (2) About two miles from here.
   A. Mode (3) Near where we saw that accident yester-
        day.

An answer in any one mode can be further pursued by specific requests for a translation into another mode. It is expected that in general these requests will be in the direction of mode (1), e.g. for answers in modes (2) and (3), 'Where exactly is that?'

Other interrogatives might be used to specify which mode of answer (1) or (2) is required.

   e.g. for Mode (1) In which street, town, etc., does John Smith live?
   for Mode (2) How far from here does John Smith live?

There does not appear to be another interrogative which specifies that the answer is required to be given in mode (3).

3   When

'When' shares many of the features of 'where', but refers to time. The information to be given in the structure of a replacement adverbial group or clause locates an event in time.

Four modes have been separated for answers to 'when' questions: (1) specification in terms of BC/AD, month, day, hour, etc.; (2) specification in terms of time from the present; (3) specification in terms of personal age; (4) specification in terms of another event.*

The 'extra' mode which has no parallel for 'where' questions is mode (3) referring to personal age, which would seem to be sufficiently common as an answer to certain types of question in certain contexts to justify separating it from mode (4).

---

* It is now thought that the modes suggested here have been unduly influenced by the data available. The end-points of the underlying continuum were thought of as objective—universal versus subjective-particularistic. That is, at one extreme there are time-markers and time-scales like BC/AD or the Chinese calendar or seconds, minutes and hours, that to all common intents and purposes approach universality and objectivity, while at the other extreme individuals can relate events to a time-scale which may be known only to themselves. Our mode (4) illustrates the dilemma at the other end, if we contrast the two statements, 'It was just after they landed on the moon' and 'When I was ill that time'. The first relates one event to another outside the person, but the second event is relative to personal experience. This degree of self-reference may well be important in both developmental and social psychology.

Example: Q. When did you go to Italy last?
A. Mode (1) In 1962.
Mode (2) Six years ago.
Mode (3) When I was twenty.
Mode (4) The year before I went to Spain.

An answer given in one mode may, as for 'where', be pursued to obtain an answer in a different mode. Answers in modes (3) and (4) could quite commonly be further pursued with 'And when was that?' or 'And when were you twenty?', each further question moving towards (2) or (1). (2) could be pursued with 'And which year is it now?', but this is unlikely, or 'And which year was that?' which is not so improbable. (1) could be reiterated for greater precision with 'And when in 1962?' but this request for precision is not one for a change of mode. Other interrogatives may be used to specify the mode required (also see the example above) for pursuing an answer in mode (2) for modes (1), (2) and (3).

e.g. for Mode (1) In which year did you go to Italy last?
Mode (2) How long ago was it that you last went to Italy?
Mode (3) How old were you when you last went to Italy?

In parallel with 'where' questions, there seems to be no other interrogative which specifies that the answer be given in terms of some other event.

4 How

'How' has a variety of meanings, giving different modes of *question* (p. 5). Because 'how' has a greater variety of answers than the interrogative words examined earlier, an exposition of possible coding of some sample answers is given. For the first two modes we illustrate the use of a compound use of 'how', where 'how' has a modifying function within a larger group, rather than being the sole exponent of the group, and specifies the referential category, 'degree'.

Modes

Mode 1: Verb ascriptive. 'How' is used to introduce requests for evaluative or descriptive information about states or values of attributes of persons or objects, and the predicator is expounded by an ascriptive verb.

In the simple type (*a*) a whole new intensive complement is required in the answer:

e.g. (1*a*) Q. How are you?
    A. I am *well* or I am *happy*.

In the compound type (*b*) some modification or intensification of a complement already supplied is requested:

e.g. (1*b*) Q. How long is the wall?
    A. The wall is *ten miles* long.

Mode 2: Verb non-ascriptive. The second mode requires an evaluation of an activity by means of an adverbial group. In the compound question (2*b*) an intensification of the adverb already supplied is required:

e.g. (2*a*) Q. How did it go?
    A. It went *terribly*.
   (2*b*) Q. How well do you ski?
    A. I ski *very* well.

Mode 3. This is a question which asks for information about a process, method, or a specification of the relations between two or more events; often a causal sequence is required.

e.g. (3) Q. How do you ride a bicycle?
    A.(i) First of all you sit on the saddle with one foot on the ground. Then you put your hands on the handlebars and then . . . etc. (describing process).
    A.(ii) One rides a bicycle *by pedalling*.

Whether 3 (i) or 3 (ii) is given in reply will depend in part upon the context of the question and hence the answerer's interpretation of its intention. The possible use of the adjunctive 'by . . .' construction will also depend upon the availability of verbal nouns or named methods which can be used for a precise summary of some complex activity or process.

Mode 4. This mode is the theme predicated type of 'how' question— requiring an explanation of an activity or occurrence.

e.g. (4) Q. How is it that John always gets here first?
    A. It is because *John is the keenest one here*.

This mode is very similar to a 'why' question and is likely to evoke a similar range of answers.

5 Why

There do not appear to be such linguistically specifiable required structures for answers to 'why' questions as there are for most other interrogatives. There are some likely grammatical and lexical choices, e.g. that of the conditioning clause beginning with 'because', and negatively there are structures and lexical items which would provide replacement groups for other interrogatives and yet be inappropriate here.

We have separated more modes of answering for 'why' questions than for any other type. Like the fourth question mode of 'how', 'why' demands an explanation. Explanation is a complicated concept, but for present purposes it is suggested that an adequate explanation can best be defined in terms of what satisfies the questioner: explanation is subjective rather than objective. A contextually adequate explanation could be defined operationally in terms of the questioner not continuing to ask a further 'why' question of the explanation offered. However, there are objections to this. The questioner may cease to reiterate the 'why' question because he feels he will not be able to extract a satisfactory answer from the respondent or because the answerer may tell the questioner to stop asking the question and threaten him. A more satisfactory definition of contextual adequacy would be in terms of the questioner not wishing to ask further 'why' questions, but this may be more difficult to measure.

It is presumed that a 'why' question is asked when the person does not understand some event or relationship between events. Answers are adequate if they persuade the questioner that the event questioned is an example of some other principle that the questioner already understands or accepts as true. An explanation then involves demonstrating that the content of the question is a member of a set of acceptable propositions. Two aspects are involved: one is finding a principle that the questioner would accept as an explanation, and the other requirement to be satisfied is that the answerer convince the questioner that his question is an example of this principle. (Modes are possibly acceptable principles.)

The search for a classification of modes could have been based on either linguistically or psychologically interesting distinctions. In fact, neither was accorded a superior emphasis. A sample of questions and possible answers was drawn up, and both linguistic and psychological considerations were held in mind during the attempt to divide this set into categories. The exposition of the differences among the categories chosen gives a brief description and examples of each, followed by a mention of linguistic structures and elements which may serve to identify the mode. 'Because' is the omnibus binder, whose presence is a sufficient condition for recognizing at the least an implicit 'why' question, but its use is not obligatory and does not discriminate among modes of answer.

The first two modes are not really modes at all. They have no explanatory value and might be better viewed as inappropriate answers of some sort, but since both are frequently used as effective replies they are included.

(i) Denial of oddity

A 'why' question is normally asked when the questioner is ignorant of the reasons for an event occurring or finds a particular event unusual. 'Why did they *walk* down the street?' is most likely to be asked if the questioner has seen the event as exceptional and not part of an accepted sequence of events. The exceptional feature of the event will be marked orally by stress. The most distinctive form of the denial of oddity is 'Why shouldn't . . . ?', a repetition of the question with its A P(S) structure and a negated modal verb. We do not normally regard such a reply as an answer at all (see p. 23). There are other answers with a similar function: '*Everyone* knows that (why)', 'It's *not unusual* (strange, odd, etc.)', 'There's *nothing unusual* (strange, etc.) about that', 'I *don't* see what's *unusual* (strange, etc.) about that'. Grammatically, these answers have structures indistinguishable from those of other modes and it is only in lexis that distinguishing features occur. All but one of the examples have a complement expounded by an epithet referring to rarity and somewhere in the structure a negation of this rarity is made. This is not necessarily achieved by a verb with negative polarity. The other is the affirmative obverse of the explicit denials. This is the only mode where 'because' could not reasonably be used to introduce the answer.

(ii) Restatement of question

It is possible simply to restructure the content of a question like 'Why do leaves fall from trees?', substitute a 'because' for the 'why' and reply, '*Because they do*'. An alternative tactic is to perform a similar restructuring with or without the 'because' substitution and insert an adjunct of limitation, such as 'just', e.g. 'They *just* do'. Grammatically, this second way of producing the mode gives a clause structure SP (C) with an adverbial insertion, usually SAP; this form seems to be confined to this mode and appeals to emotions or wishes (mode (6)). The first means has no grammatical uniqueness, and it is only when the question has been specified that the lexical cues for identification become available. However, it is common for the answer to show lexical and minimal grammatical presupposition, e.g. 'They just do'.

(iii) Appeal to regularity

(a) *APPEAL TO REGULARITY (GENERAL)*

For a particular event or for an event whose regularity is not made explicit, an explicit appeal to its regularity can be made:

e.g. Q. Why do the leaves fall off the trees?
A. They fall *every* winter.
A. They *always* do.

This is a weak explanation similar to a denial of oddity, but without its double negation. No grammatical features differentiate this category, but lexically some adverb or epithet of frequent, usual, or regular occurrence will often be present.

(b) *APPEAL TO REGULARITY (TRADITION)*

The decision to divide this category to give a subcategory of 'tradition' was taken for social psychological reasons only. Such answers as 'Because we have always done it that way' and 'It was good enough for my father and it's good enough for me' are included in this subcategory. Although this subcategory has no more force than any other appeal to regularity, an acceptance of its applicability to social situations can be a powerful opposition to social change.

(iv) Appeal to essence

If the capacity of cows to yield milk is explained by a claim that it is part of the nature of cows to give milk, the explanation rests on the definition or connotation of 'cow'. Any claim that the link between two features depends on one feature being a defining or criterial attribute of the other (to use the modern jargon for a very old idea) constitutes an appeal to essence and converts the original question into a tautological truth. Typical answers are: 'Cows are like that', 'They wouldn't be cows if they didn't', 'It is only natural for cows to give milk', 'It's human nature', 'Boys will be boys'. These answers have no common, distinctive grammatical or lexical features, although the negative conditioning dependent clause combined with a free clause and a negative verb (the second example) is unlikely to occur in any other mode except consequence. At the lexical level the occurrence of words like 'nature', 'essence' and 'meaning' are signs of this category.

(v) Appeal to authority

Appeals to authority are more common for the regulation and explanation of social behaviour than for the illumination of problems in the physical world, although they can be used for those as well. They require the citation of a person or a rule of a system; 'Because I say so', 'Because it is the law', 'Because you have to'. Answers which could be classified here can vary along the power-authority dimension, from an abrupt command based on might through to an explicit set of reasons specifying, justifying and legitimizing the authority claimed. It may be necessary later to subdivide this category into subcategories of persons versus sets of rules, observable versus transcendental authorities, specified versus unspecified authorities, especially since these appeals are a major means of socializing children into a social structure. Such appeals will normally have a nominal group specifying the authority, and/or a verbal group which either contains 'to be' or a verb of communication, demand or compulsion. These appeals are frequently used to justify imperatives or commands that have been temporarily questioned or defied.

(vi) Appeal to emotions and wishes

Where a person has to justify a behavioural preference, he can make an immediate appeal to his likes and dislikes, wants and needs, or those of others in so far as they are seen as determining action, e.g. 'I like it' or 'I want it'. Such appeals will have a simple, but not unique, grammatical form and may have adverbs of limitation, such as 'just' or 'simply'. This will give an SP(C) structure with an inserted A. They are identified at the lexical level by verbal groups (or, rarely, nominal groups) of affect or conation. This category will occur only for a limited range of 'why' questions concerned with human behaviour.

(vii) Explanation by analogy

An explanation by analogy cites a set of events, objects or processes which are already assumed to be understood and points to the parallels between this understood situation and the current problem, e.g. '(Blood in the body), *It is like* oil in a car'. Grammatically, 'it is' is likely to precede an adverbial group expounded by a preposition and complement. Lexically, words such as 'like', 'similar', 'the same as' will be used to link the explicand and the explicator.

(viii) Categorization

To give an object, event or process a name or to categorize it more generally can serve as an explanation. 'It is a case of projection', offered as a reason for a person's racial prejudice, may be a contextually adequate explanation, provided that the questioner understands 'projection' and can see how this particular example comes to be placed under this heading. If either of these conditions is not met, the explanation is debased. It is not uncommon in social science to attach an undefinable label to a particular phenomenon and assume that an explanation has been given. This weak labelling is like an appeal to essence, but a successful inclusion of a phenomenon under a widely accepted set of propositions, which accounts for much else besides, is considered a high form of explanation (Braithwaite, 1953).

At a later stage it will be necessary to differentiate between simple same-level labelling and other grades of categorization. The labelling will often include an anaphoric 'it' with 'to be', followed by 'a case', 'an instance', 'an example' and 'of' with a nominal group defining the category, e.g. 'It's a case of arthritis', 'It's an example of Parkinson's Law'. This category can often be identified grammatically and lexically for simple answers.

(ix) Cause- (x) effect explanations

A distinction is drawn between consequence and cause. If we ask why leaves fall off the trees in winter and the answer specifies the antecedents or origins of this event, the answer can be referred to as 'causal'. A causal explanation specifies processes or events *prior in time* to those to be explained. On the other hand, the answer could specify the consequences or results of the leaves falling off, and one type of consequence can be the purpose or function of the leaves falling. In this case the explanation is in terms of events which could occur *in the future*, if the leaves did or did not fall. With human behaviour it is probably only when the consequences are *intended* that a purposive explanation is permissible, but with non-human objects, processes or events no such requirement is made, and the satisfactoriness of a functional or teleological explanation is implied. An appeal to consequence treats the event as the cause of some future effect, whereas a causal explanation treats it as an effect of past causes. It is probably safer and more comprehensively valid to call those cause-effect explanations which make future reference 'appeals to consequence' rather than 'appeals to purpose'.

The above differences between 'cause' and 'consequence' modes are not difficult to specify linguistically and the following list of binders separate the two types:

(ix) Causal	Either	(x) Consequence
since	because	in order to
owing to	for	in order that
due to	for the sake of	so that
on account of		so as to
as a result of		to + non-finite verb
as a consequence of		

When 'because' is used as an introductory binder, a wide variety of structures can follow. A counter-factual hypothetical structure, i.e. 'If not . . . then . . .', will not occur as a causal explanation, but can as an appeal to consequence. However, in general, reliance has to be placed upon lexical indications of the temporal relationships of events.

Any one answer to a 'why' question can involve pure examples of these modes or mixtures of them. The distinctions among the categories are not so clear as they might be, and new categories may be required as a result of extended experience. Further, any systematic attempts to compare the worth of the different types of explanation will have to wait until the scheme for coding according to mode has been applied. Subcategories devised to cope with the problem of evaluating the explanations falling within a category were suggested by the data available (see Vol. II). It will be necessary to divide reasons into true and false (appropriateness), to rate the fullness of the explanation (completeness), and to assess the validity of presuppositions made, but the complexities involved are such that they are best examined within the confines of the sets of answers produced in particular empirical investigations.

6 Which and What

'Which' and 'what' are the two interrogative words most commonly used to serve within the referential categories normally associated with other interrogative words. 'Which' before nouns referring to persons can substitute for 'who' and can be used, for instance, before the words 'time', 'place' and 'manner' to substitute for 'when', 'where' and 'how'. 'What' too can be used as a modifier (though in some cases, some may say, incorrectly) or a complement, so that 'What man . . .?' 'What is that man?' is equivalent to some uses of 'who', 'What time . . .?' or 'What is the time . . .?' to 'when'; 'What place . . .?' to 'where'; 'What makes . . .?' is sometimes interpreted as a 'how' process question; 'What is the explanation . . .?' as a 'how' explanation question or a 'why' question.

These two interrogatives do, however, function in unique ways to obtain answers, whether within their own normal referential categories or those associated with other interrogative words, and we shall examine this now, albeit only briefly.

(i) Which

The nominal head following 'which' specifies a set of objects and attributes, etc., and an appropriate, complete answer requires a unique identification of the preferred member of the set specified. As we have shown for 'who', 'when' and 'where', here too an answer involving inadequate presupposition may be pursued for greater precision.

e.g. (1) Which restaurant?
The Indian restaurant.
(2) Which Indian restaurant?
Ye Olde Bombaye Ducke.

In some cases, e.g. 'Which method of analysis shall we use?', there may be no unique one-word label and a descriptive account may be necessary. (The existence or non-existence of a single label is possibly a function of the frequency with which the category has been and is referred to and may be an example of Zipf's law on abbreviation (1935).)

(ii) What

'What' differs from 'which' in that the set from which an answer is to be drawn is less well defined (that is, unless 'what' is used in the same way as 'which' for the modification of a noun). Where 'what' alone forms the interrogative group, the specification or definition required may be of either (a) an object (nominal group), or (b) an activity (verbal group).

e.g. (a) What do you see?
(b) (one use of) What are you doing? This requires the substitute verb 'do' to be replaced by a more specific entry.

When used in combination with 'sort of' or 'kind of' as a modifier, it requires the specification of a smaller set from the larger set expressed in the nominal group head.

e.g. What kind of dog is that?

When used in combination with 'like' it has greater possibilities for description than 'how' mode (1) in its simple form, which is generally confined to the state of a person. 'What like' can include the meaning expressed in 'how' mode (1).

e.g. What are you feeling like?

However, 'what like' referring to activity is functionally close to 'how' mode (2) (manner):

e.g. What does he ski like?

F

Chapter 4   Restricted and elaborated codes and answering

1   Relevant features of Bernstein's theory

A brief statement of Bernstein's theoretical position has been given in Chapter I: that the lower working class in Britain is generally confined to a 'restricted' code of language use which functions mainly to maintain or change the nature of role relationships, while the middle class, as well as using language for this function, will also possess an 'elaborated' code which functions to talk and write, listen or read about the physical and social world in which man lives.

It is outside the frame of reference of this monograph to review the current status of the theory; neither does it seem appropriate to cite the accumulating mass of evidence consistent with Bernstein's views. Our immediate concern is to examine how Bernstein's ideas apply to the answer aspect of the question-answer exchange. What should be the differences in the answers of restricted and elaborated code users to 'wh' questions in terms of the categories expounded in Chapters 2 and 3?

According to Bernstein, the major features of the lower-working-class restricted code relevant to answers to 'wh' questions are:

1   Users of the code are not oriented towards an optimal reliance upon language as a vehicle for informing or instructing others or themselves in a knowledge or understanding of the physical and social world. The potential uses of language for learning, problem-solving, ordering and systematizing, skill acquisition, etc., are not seen. There is a failure to grasp the full import of the referential usage of language: that to talk usefully about the world there must be a correspondence between declarative sentences uttered and the non-verbal world to which they are referring.

2   The restricted code user assumes a near identity of experience between himself and others. Although his language may have the formal facilities for taking other points of view, these possibilities are not manifested.

3 As far as structure is concerned, there will be less concern about generally accepted (or pedagogically prescribed) morphological and syntactical rules. These will be simplified at the ranks of morpheme, word, group, clause and sentence. Sentences are likely to be well-rehearsed invariant sequences, composed of chunks, clichés or proverbs, more reminiscent of Skinner's (1957) than Chomsky's (1957) views about language.

4 The restricted-code user will be more concerned to point out the immediately observable than discuss the absent and abstract. Hence the lexical items will tend to have concrete rather than abstract referents, and will be few in number, since their use can be supplemented by non-verbal behaviour. The grammatical structure, particularly at the rank of group (nominal, verbal, adverbial) and higher can also be simple for the same reason.

5 The restricted-code user will not be interested in the explanation of events and processes, and his language will therefore tend to lack the generally accepted linguistic features associated with explanations.

These separations are neither discrete nor exhaustive, but do help focus attention upon the general hypotheses advanced in the rest of this chapter and empirically tested in Chapters 5, 6 and 7.

2 Derivative hypotheses applied to answering

(i) Context

At the level of contextual meaning, a question will be seen by an elaborated-code user to have a greater number of potential meanings to be eliminated by considerations of the relevant situational categories. This does not mean that both an elaborated- and a restricted-code user may not each arrive at the same appropriate instantial meanings, although the restricted-code user's bias towards an interpretation in terms of social role relationships should lead him to attend unduly to indicators falling within the residual scale of register, i.e. features indicative of the attitudes and emotions of the questioner, particularly those relevant to the immediate role relationship. He is therefore less likely to sense possible varieties of questions, prone to make a social interpretation of them, and because his attention is also upon the paralinguistic features, he may be more likely not to hear the actual question when it is posed under noisy conditions or when questions are difficult. Whether there are effects upon his answers will depend upon the experimental conditions, but at least the direction in which any errors should occur can be predicted.

Along the scales of register, field, role, formality, and medium we would expect an elaborated-code user to make more differentiation in the language used across all four. Limitation to a restricted code, although separating registers in response to situational categories, will probably lead to possible differences becoming less distinct. There should be less apparent consciousness of the demarcations between fields of discourse and less flexibility in switching appropriately across these fields, with a lack of awareness that, for example, not only are words used in different technical senses in different disciplines, but that they are also associated with different syntactic rules (for example, the linguist's use of 'role' is rather different than that of the social psychologist, and we twitch imperceptibly each time we use it, feeling that 'function' would be more appropriate). For role (function!) the restricted-code user will tend to converge upon a social one, not only in the decoding mentioned above, but also in the answers given, emphasizing authority, with a reliance upon commands expressed overtly in imperative sentences and declarative sentences with prescriptive modal verbs (must, etc.) and covertly in other ways, and emphasizing sentiments with a variety of verbal forms of expression. Style will tend towards the informal, and the communication of the restricted-code user should be most efficient in a face-to-face medium with considerable opportunity for immediate feedback where agreement can be checked and paralinguistic features exploited. Speech will be handled better than writing.

As far as answering is concerned, the implications are that the restricted-code user will be most effective as a communicator in informal face-to-face situations where speech is to be used, but it is in just such settings that he will tend to exploit non-verbal ways of answering.

As far as participant features are concerned, the elaborated-code user will tend to allow for possible differences in states of knowledge and belief between speaker and listener and make few assumptions of similarity where these are as yet unknown. According to Bernstein's theory, a restricted-code user will tend to assume that the other person is very similar to himself and answer accordingly. The restricted code can be seen to be more likely than the elaborated code to lead to *contextual presupposition* of an inappropriate kind—in this case too much.

We would like to add a rider to this view. The restricted-code user is also aware of the distinction between 'them' and 'us', and this might mean that when he identifies his protagonist as one of 'them' he may be prone to exaggerate the dissimilarity, with a consequent under-estimation of what would be valid *contextual presupposition*, so that in this instance he will make too little.

Finally, under context we need to consider questions requiring factual information about persons, objects, events and process; the elaborated-code user should be able to supply fuller information (*contextual completeness*), since he is oriented more toward the outside world and can be said to be more concerned with processes and events outside his immediate experience than is the restricted-code user. This should also lead to a higher probability of the information that is given being true (*contextually appropriate*) if the elaborated code also functions to relate one appropriately to the 'real world'.

(ii) Mode

Where the context allows for different modes of response, those chosen by the elaborated-code user should generally be more objective and more concerned to set the thesis of the question outside the framework of subjective experience, and into the network of its relations in the 'real world'. The greater coverage of the events, processes, objects outside its user that is characteristic of the elaborated code contrasts with an acceptance of these as given and unproblematic by the restricted code.

Such differences as these should lead to a greater preference among elaborated-code speakers for the use of *objective* modes in answer to 'when' and 'where' questions, for instance, while confinement to the restricted code will predispose an answerer to reply in terms of his own personal reference system, e.g. for space: his home, place of work, town or present location; for time: his own age, event in his own past, the present time, or ages of and events in the lives of close friends and relatives. When a personal reference system is used as a first answer to a 'when' or 'where' question, the elaborated-code user should find it easier than a restricted-code speaker to reorganize the information into a more objective reference system.

Bernstein (1961) argues that restricted-code users should have particular difficulty with 'why' questions. Many 'why' questions, particularly those asked of parents by children and those about social or moral matters, are likely to be construed as challenges to established authority. Power can be reasserted by the use of *a repetition of the question as an answer, denials of oddity*, and *appeals to authority, essence* and *regularity*. Proverbs may also play a role in this interaction, and although we do not know what happens in Britain, the device is widely exploited in other cultures (Arewa and Dundas, 1964).

In mode selection an elaborated-code user will show a preference for presenting information about conditions and events antecedent to or consequent upon the thesis of the question or about relevant characteristics of and relations between participants in an event. Such information is conveyed in *causal* and *consequence modes*. There may be an attempt to raise the discussion to a higher level of generality by the use of *categorization* or to make a point more clearly by use of *analogy*.

(iii) Form

Since for the restricted-code user the linguistic content of an utterance is of relatively less concern than for the elaborated-code person, while paralinguistic and certain extra-linguistic features may receive more attention, we may discover differences in the form in which the users of the two codes answer questions. Under conditions of minimal difficulty no differences should emerge, but as question-answer exchanges move away from clichés and habitual sequences and the answers become more difficult to construct, the elaborated-code user should give answers which are more *appropriate grammatically and lexically* in each of the three answer areas of *core*, *concordance* and *residue* (Chapter 2.)

Where a replacement group is used in an answer, the elaborated-code user should be more able to supply a *grammatically* and *lexically complete* answer.

Greater flexibility with language may result in more *grammatical presupposition*, where the situation allows the elaborated-code user to do so without a loss of necessary information. The same considerations apply to *lexical presupposition*.

Comment

As we have already stated, we do not intend to test all or even most of the predictions that can be derived. In particular, we omit variations at the contextual level, concentrating our efforts upon mode and form. With what degree of success the next three chapters show.

Chapter 5   Answers of five-year-old children to 'wh' questions*

A preliminary application of the scheme of analysis

I   Introduction

Four hundred and forty children in two socially distinct London boroughs were required to perform six tasks, designed to give a useful and varied sample of the speech of five-year-olds. One function of the data is to provide a grammatical and lexical description of the speech, and it is hoped that an internal analysis of these linguistic variables will generate higher-order concepts similar to Bernstein's 'elaborated' and 'restricted' codes; in turn, variation in such scores will be linked to their sociological and social-psychological antecedents.

One problem not dealt with in the main analysis is the linguistic and psychological variation of answers to questions. A detailed system (Chapters 2 and 3) has been developed which classifies answers by appropriateness, completeness and amount of presupposition at the levels: grammar, lexis, mode and context. It is most useful when answers contain only one or a few sentences, whereas most of the questions asked of the children in this setting were intended to evoke much longer utterances. However, questions in three tasks were selected for a preliminary analysis to see whether the coding frame had any empirical validity and to see if there were social or psychological variables related to differences in the answers given. As the actual analysis shows, this particular system was found to be less appropriate for the data in hand than a simpler linguistic and content analysis. The questions examined were:

* This chapter is virtually identical to the article published by Rackstraw, S. J. and Robinson, W. P. 'Social and psychological factors related to variability of answering behaviour in five-year-old children'. *Language and Speech* (1967), x, 88–106.

(i) At the end of answering what was happening in three detailed paintings by Trotin, each child was asked, 'What shall we call this picture? What name shall we give it?'

(ii) For a game which he had said he liked playing, each child had to answer 'How do you play that game?' and was given one probe, 'How does it start?' or 'How does it go on?'

(iii) After each child had described the actions of a toy elephant which nodded its head, played cymbals, banged a drum, and moved along the table-top when a rubber bulb was squeezed, he was asked, 'How does it work?', followed by 'What makes it work?'

The details of the scoring are given separately for each task. It was generally expected that middle-class and high-intelligence test-score children would give answers of a more complex nature, more appropriate linguistically both at the grammatical and lexical levels, and that they would presuppose more of the question in their answers. Such children are more likely to have been exposed to an elaborated code; they should be more competent at learning it and have more opportunity for its use. One aim of the wider project is to isolate the social-psychological characteristics of social class responsible for the separation of children into elaborated- and restricted-code users, and an early attempt to do this was called a 'communication index': this was added to the analysis conducted here. In addition, the precaution has been taken of dealing with boys and girls separately.

2 Method

Subjects

For two tasks the subjects used comprised the 80 children from the high- and medium-intelligence test-score groups of a factorial sample which had a two-way division on sex, social class and communication index and a three-way division on verbal intelligence scores, with five children in each cell (see Table 1). For the analysis of the game (Question 2) the factorial sample proved to be unsatisfactory. The children had been offered a choice of explaining how to play one of three games: 'Hide-and-seek', 'Musical chairs' and 'Ring-a-ring-o'-roses'. These games differ structurally and the analysis was restricted to 'Hide-and-seek'. The number of factorial subjects who both chose this game and were given the correct questions and probes by the interviewers was too small to permit a statistical analysis, and so the total sample of children was examined: 28 boys were found such that 7 were high-I.Q. (English Picture Vocabulary Test scores > 112) middle class, 7 high-I.Q. working class, 7 medium-I.Q. (E.P.V.T. score < 113) middle class and 7 medium-I.Q. working class, and all had been given the correct initial question.

Indices

Social class was coded as an equally weighted sum of each parent's occupation and schooling. The correlation with a simple Hall-Jones social-class scale was very high. Middle-class subjects have both parents in Hall-Jones, 1, 2 or 3, or their parents are in lower-middle-class occupations, but have more than basic secondary education. Subjects who have parents with basic secondary education only and come into Hall-Jones 5 form the upper limit of the working class, but most of the working-class children included are of parents in semi- or un-skilled jobs with only basic secondary education.

The communication index was an early estimate on a ten-point scale of the extent to which the mother talks to the child. It is based upon two short questionnaires: the first specified seven situations (e.g. around the house, trying to relax, in a shop) and the mother indicated on a four-point scale her willingness to respond verbally to the child's attempt to chatter to her; the second was a five-way multiple choice, for which the mother indicated on a three-point frequency scale her response to the child's difficult questions (e.g. try to change the subject, tell him as much as you can). A correlational and varimax factor analysis on the total sample showed that

TABLE 5.1 *Composition of sample*

Task: Picture title and toy elephant

| | High I.Q. | | Medium I.Q. | |
	High comm. Index	Low comm. Index	High comm. Index	Low comm. Index
Middle-class boys	5	5	5	5
Middle-class girls	5	5	5	5
Working-class boys	5	5	5	5
Working-class girls	5	5	5	5

Task: Explanation of game. Boys only

	High I.Q.	Medium I.Q.
Middle-class	7	7
Working-class	7	7

a general factor underlies both schedules, and the final index utilized all items. This index has subsequently been revised, but the experimental design used here had already utilized this early version.

The intelligence test score categories defined 'high' as being at the 90th percentile or higher on the Crichton Vocabulary Scale, 'medium' as 50th to 75th and 'low' as 25th or below (Raven, 1949). Eleven children in the sample (10 per cent) deviate from this criterion, but such deviants made appropriate scores on a second test, the English Picture Vocabulary Test (Brimer and Dunn, 1962). Only the high and medium groups were used here.

Treatment of results

A four-way comparison was made wherever possible between middle and working class, high and medium intelligence test scores, boys and girls, and high and low communication index. The basic strategy was to compare the relative proportions of children in the opposed groups using a particular type of answer. Where expected cell frequencies were below five, and a one-sample comparison was required, the binominal test was used. Where a 2×2 table resulted and cell frequencies were low, the Fisher Exact Probability Test was used, otherwise a x^2 test was run.

3a Toy elephant: scoring procedure

For the explanation of the workings of the toy elephant, two questions were asked; first, 'How does it work?' and, second, 'What makes it work?'

How does it work?

At the time the analysis was made the distinctions mentioned in Chapters 2 and 3 had not been made, but it is possible to relate the actual scoring to the final distinctions achieved. The question is a mode (3) 'How' question, for which we differentiated between 3 (i) principle and 3 (ii) process explanations. The children's answers implied the possible usefulness of a distinction within process, viz. mechanical versus procedure, while it was necessary to include a further category of demonstration. Since the experimenter was blindfolded, this form of explanation was not appropriate to the situation, but it was rather optimistic to expect five-year-olds to comprehend the nature of this task. Some children made no attempt at explaining, but just described the elephant's activity—again an inappropriate answer, this time in terms of mode; they were in fact answering, 'What is the elephant doing?'

Definitions of scoring categories:

(1) *No answer* or 'I don't know'.

(2) *Description:* This was scored if there was only a simple narration of what the toy did or could be made to do, e.g. 'He's banging the drum and playing the cymbals with his trunk'.

(3) *Explanation*
   (*a*) Demonstration: This was where the child performed the necessary actions to make the toy work, accompanying them with a brief comment, e.g. 'Like this'.
   (*b*) Process—mechanical: While the experimenter's intention was to evoke an attempt at explaining all the elephant's behaviour, some children offered a partial causal explanation: only that the cymbals banged because they were moved by his head, e.g. 'His head goes up and down and bangs the cymbals'.
   (*c*) Process—procedure: This was similar to the mechanical-process explanation, but the child stated what the *operator* had to do to make the toy work, e.g. 'You have to press this red thing and then it works. With the red thing.'
   (*d*) Principle: When the explanation referred to a general scientific concept, 'principle' was scored, e.g. 'By air pressure', 'By electricity'.

An answer could be coded under more than one category.

(*a*) COMPLETENESS

Grammar and Context   Answers were graded for structural linguistic completeness: 4, explicitly complete (marked often by 'and that's how it works'); 3, implicitly complete (a conventually sufficient answer, but no explicit statement of completeness); 2, partial completeness; 1, minimal. The degree of completeness was coded for both descriptions and explanations.

Lexis   Answers were scored for lexical completeness and delicacy, and in those answers referring to the small, red rubber bulb which had to be pressed, a graduation was made of explicitness: 1, 'this' or some other ostensive definition, 2, 'thing', 'something', 3, ostensive definition qualified by 'little', 'red', etc., 4, 'thing' qualified with 'little', 'red', etc., 5, noun, such as 'balloon', 'handle', 'pusher'.

(b) *TRUTH OF ANSWER*

Answers were classified as; true, 3, partially true, 2, false, 1.

(c) *LINGUISTIC STRUCTURE*

Answers were analysed in terms of Halliday's Scale and Category Grammar (see Turner and Mohan, 1970) and the following categories were used:

1	A(pc)	Model answer: By pressing the bulb
2	F1 (SPC)	Model answer: You press the handle
3	F1(SPC)+F1(SP) etc.	Model answer: You press the handle and it works
4	F1(Z)B2(SPC)	Model answer: A little bulb which sends the air
5	Z or A	Model answer: That
6	F3(PC)	Model answer: Press the bulb

What makes it work?

A cursory examination of the answers to the question suggested that the analysis used for 'How does it work?' was superfluous here. Since the actual classification employed gave no significant differences, it will not be described in detail: it separated types of feature referred to (e.g. bulb, squeak, pressing) and the linguistic structures used.

Predictions

It was expected that high-communication-index, high-I.Q., middle-class children would be more likely to give complete, true explanations of 'how' with a preference for an explanation in terms of principle. The answers to the 'how' questions may have influenced the answer to 'what' and the results were simply examined for differences, but it was expected that references to the red rubber bulb should be more explicit and less ostensive in the middle-class, high-I.Q., high-communication-index groups.

3b Toy elephant: results

HOW DOES IT WORK?

Tabulations by sex, social class, intelligence test scores and communication index revealed no significant differences among groups. Only the social class distributions are given (see Table 5.2). Table 5.3 shows the grammatical structure of answers. The cell numbers were reduced for the working class by twelve incorrectly posed questions. One difference which might have achieved significance with more subjects was the middle class tendency to give more concise (less 'complete') answers. The working class often used more than one

TABLE 5.2 *Variations in mode, completeness and truth of answer by social class*

| | Social class | |
	Middle class	Working class
Mode		
(1) Description	5	2
(2) Explanation		
(*a*) Mechanical	2	4
(*b*) Principle	1	2
(*c*) Procedure	28	22
(*d*) Demonstration	4	2
(3) Don't know or no answer	2	12
Total	42	44
Completeness		
High 4	7	8
3	23	13
2	7	7
Low 1	1	0
No answer	2	12
Total *n*	40	40
Truth of answer		
High 3	29	21
2	8	4
Low 1	1	3
No answer	2	12
Total *n*	40	40

free clause, but a further analysis showed that this contained no new information; it repeated part of the question and was generally of the form 'and it works' or 'and it goes' ($x^2 = 1{\cdot}80$). There were more 'By pressing this' constructions in the middle class ($p = 0{\cdot}022$, binomial test), especially in the high-I.Q. high-communication-index group.

TABLE 5.3 *Clause structure by social class*

Structural mode		*Social class*	
Linguistic symbols	*Examples*	*Middle-class*	*Working-class*
A(pc)	By pressing the bulb	11	2
F1(SPC)	You press the handle	11	6
F1(SPC)+F1(SP), etc.	You press the handle and it works	10	14
F1B clauses	A little bulb which sends the air	2	4
Z or A	That	3	1
F3 (PC)	Press the bulb	2	2
Question not asked or 'Don't know'		3	12
Total *n*		42*	41*

* 2 middle-class and 1 working-class subjects gave A(pc)+F1 (SP)

No distributions of variations in answers to 'What makes it work?' or the explicitness of the reference to the red rubber bulb are given, since no social differences resulted.

4a Trotin pictures: scoring procedure

The final question for the Trotin cards had two parts: 'What shall we call this picture? What name shall we give it?', the second being given directly after the first as an extra stimulus and the two together requiring a single answer. The analysis was of the content rather than the structure of the answers as the main interest shifted to how children were distributed in giving answers which were realistic descriptions of the picture rather than odd associations; another main category contrasted a summarizing title with what appeared to be the selection of a detail or details of the picture for the title. There was insufficient variation in the structure of answers to make a grammatical analysis worthwhile. The categories used for classifying answers are shown in Table 5.4.

TABLE 5.4 *Coding-frame examples*

	Picture 1	*Picture 2*	*Picture 3*
(1) *Theme*			
(a) Place	Station, platform		A town, street
(b) Event	People going on the train	The party, wedding	Shopping day
(2) *Items only* One or more than one item			
(a) Object	Train, aeroplane	Church, food	Shop, water
(b) Event	Hurrying people	Cats are on the roof	A man playing the guitar
(3) *Association*			
(a) Place	Southend/At the seaside	In England/holiday camp	Beckenham
(b) Event	Going to Auntie Betty's/war picture	Dinky Darky's party/a sword fight	London Fair/the drain's overflowing
(c) Object	Heezy Housy Train/naughty people	Princess	The River Rodin/a rose
(d) Ambiguous	Bumble down/the wrong picture	The lion roars	Sky Ray/a bedtime story
(4) *Person name*	What your name is	Eileen	Shirley
(5) *Evaluation*	Funny	It's just a picture	Pretty
(6) *Don't know* or no answer			

Predictions

It was expected that high-I.Q., high-communication-index, middle-class children would avoid the category 2, where only limited items are selected, and would move towards category 1, realistic summaries and thematic answers. They should be more likely to understand the question and hence give fewer answers in categories 4, 5 and 6, but there seemed to be no basis for expecting group differences on associative answers, 3.

4b Trotin pictures: results

Table 5.5 shows the distribution of answers, with each child having a possible score of 3, one for each picture. Although thematic answers were the most frequent, both item and association answers were common.

TABLE 5.5 *Percentage distribution of incidence of categories across three pictures*

Theme	Item	Association	Name	Evaluation	Don't know
Category					
(1a) (1b)	(2a) (2b)	(3a) (3b) (3c) (3d)	(4)	(5)	(6)
10% 25%	24% 4%	10% 7% 4% 3%	7%	1%	6%
35%	28%	24%	7%	1%	6%

$n = 240$.

To examine how groups differed from each other, binomial and x^2 tests were used.

Proportions of children using a given category

The communication index produced no suggestions of differences. I.Q. and sex yielded no statistically significant differences. High-I.Q. children used fewer event associations (3b) ($p = 0.092$) and personal names (4) ($p = 0.124$), boys used more items, objects (2a) ($p = 0.118$), event associations (3b) ($p = 0.075$) and fewer themes referring to places (1a) ($p = 0.092$), but these are suggestive only (Table 5.6). Social class gave significant discriminations in two categories: middle-class children were more likely to use themes referring to places (1a) ($p = 0.008$) and less likely to use details (2) ($p = 0.0142$; for (2a) $p = 0.011$) (Table 5.6).

TABLE 5.6 *Numbers of children, using particular categories and subcategories*

			Significance of difference
	High I.Q.	Medium I.Q.	
Category (3b)	3	10	$p = 0.092$
(4)	1	6	$p = 0.124$
	Middle-class	Working-class	
Category (1a)	13	2	$p = 0.008$
(2a)	13	25	$p = 0.075$
(2b)	2	8	$p = 0.110$
(2)	15	33	$p = 0.0142$
	Boys	Girls	
Category (1a)	4	11	$p = 0.118$
(2a)	23	15	$p = 0.075$
(3b)	10	3	$p = 0.092$

Binomial test used throughout.

The differences shown in Table 5.6 are consistent with expectations: the middle class grasped the whole picture in their title, but the working class restricted themselves to details.

Variation in the number of categories used per child over the three pictures

A count was made of the number of categories used by the child across the three pictures. Each child could use up to three categories. The 'Don't know' category was eliminated from the analysis. The results show that there was no I.Q., communication-index or sex difference. However, there were social-class differences. The middle class used fewer categories per child. Although two different types of answer per child were modal, 45 per cent of middle-class children used only one type. In the working class only 23 per cent were so consistent. Whereas 23 per cent of working-class children used three different types, only 3 per cent of the middle class did so (Table 5.7).

TABLE 5.7 *Number of categories used per child over the three pictures*

	Number of categories			
Social class	*1*	*2*	*3*	*Total*
Middle	18	21	1	40
Working	9	22	9	40
Total	27	43	10	80

$x^2 = 9.6$, $p < 0.01$

5 Explanation of game

Choice of game

Each child was given three games: Hide-and-seek, Musical Chairs and Ring-a-ring-o'-roses, from which he was to choose the one which he liked best. He was then asked to explain how to play it. For this analysis it was decided to make comparisons within one game, and Hide-and-seek was chosen for several reasons. It was the most frequently chosen game. Musical Chairs was relatively rarely chosen and appeared to be generally too difficult to receive a satisfactory explanation. Ring-a-ring-o'-roses had few stages, and answers were frequently little more than a recitation of the jingle. Only the

G

answer to the first question, 'I can't play that game. Can you tell me how to play it?' was analysed.

Hide-and-seek: scoring procedure

Although the precise nature of the version of Hide-and-seek described differed from child to child, all variants contained certain basic elements, and these provided a framework for the analysis. There are two emphases in the analysis; the first is upon the described structure of the game, while the second is concerned with the players. These two emphases converge in the question of type of description, universal or particular.

(a) THE STRUCTURE OF GAME DESCRIBED

The tabulations gave: (1) a count of the number of stages mentioned, as well as information as to which stages were recounted, (2) the temporal sequences of the stages described and the extent to which the temporal sequences of the game played and its verbal exposition were congruent. The two other features noted were: (3) whether or not a summary of the game was given and (4) whether the game was described in a general way or with reference to particular examples (which, as we have seen, is also concerned with the second emphasis of the analysis).

The coding frame for scoring these categories was as follows:

(1) *The game was divided into the following stages*

1 Roles division and selection (hiders and seeker).
2 Opportunity for hiding (seeker hides eyes).
3 Means of limiting time for hiding (seeker counts and/or hiders shout, 'Ready!').
4 Hiders hide.
5 Search begins and continues.
6 Seeker finds or fails to find.
7 Selection of new seeker.
8 New game begins.
9 Unusual sequences were noted.

Raw tabulations comprised a count and classification of these.

(2) *Temporal sequence of stages*

The number and nature of the deviations in the child's account from the actual temporal sequence of events listed above were noted.

(3) *Summary*   An account was called a summary when it contained a simple specification of the two essential stages in the game: (4 and 5) hiding and seeking. The child could follow the summary by some further explication, and this was noted.

(4) *Universal-particular*   The description could be both or either of universal and particular. Two children gave answers containing elements which could only be classified as 'fantasy'. This fantasy element was not given further consideration and answers were examined for elements which fell into the universal/particular categories. In order to qualify for the universal category, the explanation had to contain some linguistic marker of a non-limitation of space, time, object or persons, e.g. 'First of all you have to choose a hider. . . '.

To be counted particular, the answer had to mention a particular place or time that the game was played in or else be specific about the object used in the game or the persons playing it, e.g. 'Jim hides in our house and then we . . .' In some cases, abnormal stages were described which seemed inessential to the game and these were categorized as particular elements, e.g. 'And then we find him. We punch him.'

(b) THE PLAYERS

The second interest was in the players of the game. Here there were three foci of attention: (5) whether there was some role differentiation, i.e. division of all the players into either hiders or seekers, and (6) whether there existed some linguistic evidence or an attempt to keep these roles separate, throughout the explanation. Finally, (7) instances of linguistic inconsistency in referring to the players were noted. The sample responses varied across the total range. Some children marked the full role differentiation with distinct linguistic terms, e.g. hider versus seeker, and maintained the grammatically correct nominal and pronominal distinctions throughout. Other children initiated a distinction, but then made grammatically inaccurate or ambiguous references at a later point in the sequence, e.g. switching from 'you' to 'they'. Some children simply used 'you' or 'they' throughout for all characters and relied on non-linguistic means or no means at all for separating the roles.

The criteria used for scoring these categories were as follows:

(5) *Initial role differentiation*   A child could or could not have stated at the beginning of the explanation that it is necessary for some to hide and some to seek. This differentiation may occur as a

stage (stage 1, above) in the game or else it may occur outside the description of the process of playing. It may be in such a form as to constitute a summary of the game.

(6) *Attempts to maintain linguistic differentiation of roles* Linguistic signs which functioned to separate the roles during the explanation were noted. These were mostly nominal group modifiers and qualifiers of the actor at the head; such modifying pairs of words as 'some-other' were counted as having this function, while defining clauses as qualifiers, e.g. the one who hid, mark another instance. The use of different pronouns, e.g. you versus somebody, was not noted as functioning to separate roles, although it is realized that this may be considered an alternative method of differentiation which makes unnecessary the use of other methods.

(7) *Linguistic inconsistency in referring to players* Inconsistency was separated into (*a*) the instances where the child changed the person of the player as he proceeded through the description of the game, e.g. the seeker changed from 'somebody' to 'you', and (*b*) where it is the number that is changed, e.g. 'I' changed to 'we'.

Hide-and-seek: results

(*a*) *SELECTION OF STAGES*

Generally the social class and I.Q. groups did not differ in the number or nature of the stages they chose to include in or omit from the explanation. However, it was found that high-I.Q. boys were significantly more likely to use Stage 2 (the seeker hides his eyes) than were medium-I.Q. boys (Table 5.8) but there was no social-class difference. There was a tendency for the middle-class boys to use Stage 5 (looking for the hidden) more than the working class, but this was not significant (Table 5.8).

TABLE 5.8

	Number of boys who included stage 2				Number of boys who included stage 5		
	Middle-class	Working-class	Total		Middle-class	Working-class	Total
Medium I.Q.	2	1	3	Medium I.Q.	5	2	7
High I.Q.	4	5	9	High I.Q.	5	3	8
Total	6	6	12	Total	10	5	15

I.Q. difference, 9:3, $p = 0.05$ Class difference, 10:5

TABLE 5.9 *Summary of game present*

	Middle-class	Working-class	Total
Medium I.Q.	3	0	3
High I.Q.	3	1	4
Total	6	1	7

Class difference, 6 : 1, $p = 0.124$. No I.Q. difference.

(b) NUMBER OF STAGES

There was no social-class or I.Q. difference in the number of stages used in the answers.

(c) TEMPORAL SEQUENCE

There were no class or I.Q. differences.

(d) SUMMARY

It was found that the middle-class boys were slightly more likely to give a summary of the game (Table 5.9).

(e) UNIVERSAL-PARTICULAR TYPE OF ANSWER

There was no difference between the groups in the number of boys who gave an answer which contained some marker of universality, but there was a significant difference between the classes in the use of some particular element in the explanation (Table 5.10).

TABLE 5.10 *Number of boys using particular elements in their explanation*

	Present	Absent	Total
Middle-class	3	11	14
Working-class	10	4	14
Total	13	15	28

$p = 0.025$

The working-class were more likely to particularize and refer to specific games actually played, to times, persons and locations of such games. Among the markers of universality, some boys were found to use nouns like 'persons', 'people', etc., where others used pronouns (Table 5.11), and this was a function of social class.

TABLE 5.11 *Number of boys using nouns as markers of universality*

	At least one	None
Middle-class	8	6
Working-class	0	14

$p = 0.003$.

Middle-class boys were more likely to use universal nouns, but, further, the boys who used these nouns were mostly high-I.Q. (Table 5.12).

TABLE 5.12 *Number of high-I.Q. boys using nouns as markers of universality*

	Present	Absent
Middle-class	6	1
Working-class	0	7

$p = 0.01$

Along with their tendency to particularize, the medium-I.Q. working-class boys seemed to prefer first-person ('I', 'we') explanations more than the high-I.Q. middle class, but the numbers were too low to yield a fair test (Table 5.13).

TABLE 5.13 *Number of boys using first-person explanations*

	Middle-class	Working-class
Medium I.Q.	1	4
High I.Q.	0	1

Class difference, 5 : 1. I.Q. difference, 5 : 1.

(f) INITIAL ROLE DIFFERENTIATION

There were very few instances of initial division of players into hiders and seekers. The boys generally began straight away describing the action of the game without mentioning separately the fact of the two separate roles or the process of role selection. A few middle-class, high-I.Q. boys came close to making an initial division.

(g) THE USE OF LINGUISTIC MARKERS OF ROLE DIFFERENTIATION THROUGHOUT THE EXPLANATION

Middle-class boys were more likely to mark the role differences linguistically, but since all those who made this differentiation were in the high-I.Q. group (Table 5.14), high I.Q. was a necessary condition for the class difference to appear.

TABLE 5.14 *Number of boys marking role differentiation linguistically*

	All subjects		High-I.Q. subjects only	
	Present	*Absent*	*Present*	*Absent*
Middle-class	7	7	7	0
Working-class	0	14	0	7

Class difference $7 : 0$ $p = 0.005$

High-I.Q. middle-class children were more likely than any other group to attempt to maintain role separation.

(h) LINGUISTIC INCONSISTENCY IN REFERRING TO PLAYERS

There were no significant differences between the classes or I.Q. groups in the number of children who showed inconsistency either of person (I, he, you) or of number (singular, plural). More children (12 out of 28) made switches of person than changed number (6 out of 28). All who were inconsistent in referring to person made a mistake over the use of 'you', either using it inappropriately to replace another person or replacing it with another person. Although more middle than working class boys switched to 'you' from some other person, the numbers were too small to allow any realistic test of the possible differences.

6 Discussion

Although the analysis of linguistic structure at the rank of clause only revealed one significant difference, other indices of language competence and preference gave useful discriminations. The major operating variables of social class and I.Q. clearly have relevance to the type of answers given by the children in the sample. This is especially true of the explanation of the game and least true of the toy elephant. Sex gives no interesting differentiations, and the communication index does not emerge as a more effective discriminator than social class: unfortunately, its potential strength could not be assessed in the explanation of the game, but it did not seem to have any relevance to the other two tasks.

The failure of I.Q. and social class to be significantly related to the explanation of the working of the toy elephant is probably a function of the difficulty of the task. While most children were classified as giving true answers, this accuracy is only for a procedural account of how to work the toy (as might be expected from children of this age). Virtually none attempted an explanation of the principle, so that there was no variation in the answers to be accounted for. When these children are older, more variation in answers may occur. It is noteworthy that the linguistic clause structure had most variation in responses, and here social class differences began to appear.

Although sex, I.Q., but not the communication index, show some minor relationships to the titling of the Trotin pictures, social class produces the expected middle-class preference for thematic answers rather than those based on individual items. The incidental finding of their use of fewer categories suggests a more consistent approach to the task and a conventionally more acceptable grasp of what 'a title' should embrace.

The sample of subjects chosen for the 'Hide-and-seek' analysis gave no opportunity for examining sex and communication index differences. I.Q. becomes an important additive to social class as a discriminator among answers. The differences found suggest a greater linguistic effectiveness in the middle-class boys: they are more likely to differentiate roles linguistically and, as well as avoiding particular and concrete elements in their explanations, they use nouns rather than pronouns to achieve this effect. Finally, they are more likely to give the essential stages of the game.

There are similarities across the tasks. The summary of 'Hide-and-seek' has affinities with the 'summarizing' thematic titles on the Trotin pictures. Further, both require abstraction similar to the avoidance of descriptions of particular games of 'Hide-and-seek'. The infrequent use of first-person pronouns in the game shows an absence of self-reference similar to the use of the 'By pressing' construction with the elephant.

Probably the results can be conveniently summarized by saying that middle-class children, especially those with high I.Q. scores, approach these three tasks with speech that is less concrete and self-referential; these children are moving towards a universal objective frame of reference. Such differences are consistent with Bernstein's thesis that the 'elaborated code' can achieve greater economy in communication, greater abstraction and precision of expression and greater facility for taking an objective perspective. The economy of communication is shown by the omission of the redundant 'and that's how it works' for the elephant and by the summary of the essence of the game. The abstraction and efficiency appear in the thematic preference for a picture title, the avoidance of references to particular actual games played, the use of nouns rather than pronouns as markers of universality and the linguistic markers of role differentiation. The reduced self-reference is shown by the preference for 'persons' and rejection of first-person pronouns in the game and the preference for the adjunctive 'By pressing' construction with the elephant. The term 'self-reference' is used in preference to 'ego-centricity' because Bernstein and Piaget use this latter word in almost opposite senses. Since these results encourage us to make comparisons with Piaget's work, some explication of the different meanings attached to 'ego-centricity' and 'socio-centricity' by the two writers is required. For Piaget, 'ego-centricity' means that the young child has not yet realized the difference between himself and the rest of the world; he is not aware of perspectives other than his own. One consequence for his speech is that the child's own subjective frame of reference will predominate. It is only with the transition to socio-centric speech that the child will manifest an awareness of other points of view and use a more objective form of speech. Bernstein (1962) refers to 'ego-centric and socio-centric sequences' (originally called 'sympathetic circularity'): ego-centric sequences are indicated by prefatory clauses, such as 'I think', while socio-centric sequences such as 'isn't it' and 'you know' are rhetorical questions occurring as final tags to an utterance. For Bernstein, ego-centric sequences are characteristic features of speech in elaborated code, while socio-centric are more typical of speech in restricted code. Ego-centric sequences paradoxically show an awareness of points of view other than one's own and, hence, imply an objective frame of reference, but socio-centric sequences are tests of similarity of viewpoint, a check on shared subjectivity.

There are two further complications. Bernstein's restricted-code speaker assumes that other persons have the same knowledge, beliefs and experience as himself: he can therefore express himself subjectively using himself as a reference-point, and still expect to be understood. This means that his speech will have similarities to what Piaget calls ego-centric speech. It could be argued that Bernstein's young restricted-code user may not ever fully relinquish Piaget's first stage of ego-centric speech, because there has not been sufficient reason to do so. The other complication concerns the use of 'I' at subject. Bernstein argues that 'I' will be more common in speech in elaborated code,* particularly in the ego-centric sequences prefacing some statements. This will not be a consequence of an ego-centric viewpoint, but possibly its reverse. Because the speaker marks himself off as a unique individual, he will indicate this in his speech. The restricted-code speaker may substitute 'we' for 'I', but, following Piaget's (1926) and Vygotsky's (1962) reasoning about ego-centric speech, he may also elide the pronoun altogether.

The results obtained here do not really come under Bernstein's particular description of ego-centric and socio-centric sequences, but under his more general proposition that restricted-code users assume identity of experience with other people and will therefore retain a subjective and personal frame of reference.

The similarities to Piaget are in his distinctions between ego-centric and socio-centric speech (Piaget, 1926) and between concrete and formal operations (Piaget, 1950). The results here suggest that middle-class children, especially those with high verbal I.Q. scores, have more socio-centric speech and have at least some linguistic abilities for expressing formal operations. Piaget views both transitions as a function of age, but since age is but a representation of time available for experience and development, it is not surprising that some children 'grow up faster' than others. A Piagetian interpretation of the data would state that the middle-class children have an environment which enables their development to be accelerated relative to working-class children, and the cleverer middle-class children are able to take most advantage of this differential opportunity. The corollary is that working-class children are showing a developmental lag, both conceptually and linguistically. However, for Bernstein the subsequent development in the working-class child's speech will generally not be towards an elaborated code, e.g. working-class children of eight do not use the grammar and lexis of middle-

* The greater use of the self reference will nomally depend upon the context.

class children of six. Rather, the development will be towards adult working-class speech, so that the concrete and self-referential nature of the speech will be refined rather than reduced. If this is so, a repetition of the investigation reported here with older children of otherwise similar characteristics should continue to give similar differences and the older working-class children should not produce answers similar to those of the middle-class children of five.

Chapter 6 Answers of mothers to children's questions*

1 Introduction

The primary socializing agent for children is usually the mother. Although the child interacts with other members of the family, it is generally true in our society that most of the early interaction is with the mother. Our particular concern is with her method of dealing with children's questions. Bernstein and Brandis (Brandis and Henderson, 1970) have reported that middle-class mothers say they are more likely than working-class mothers to attempt to answer difficult questions, but here we examine in what ways answers may differ, both in quantity and quality.

Social-class differences are found, and in the discussion we try to show what the likely consequences of these are for the child. Is language playing a different role in the two social classes? Is it a means of asserting control or is it a medium of instruction? How much information of what type is transmitted to the child, and what are children likely to learn as a result of these different experiences?

Three hundred and fifty mothers of children about to enter infant school in two socially distinct London boroughs were interviewed (see Brandis and Henderson, 1970; Jones, 1966). The questions covered a wide range of topics: knowledge of and attitudes towards the educational system, the mother's role in relation to the system, her attitudes to basic skills, play, toys, painting, her methods of social control and her manner of dealing with her child's questions. Among the questions designed to give information about the verbal interaction of mother and child was a section in which the mother had to say how she would answer seven questions supposedly asked by her child: two questions asked were 'where from', one 'who', and the remaining four were 'why' questions. No explicit means of analysing the answers were devised prior to the collection of the

* This chapter first appeared in a slightly different form in *Sociology*, 1967, *i*, and is reproduced by kind permission of the Clarendon Press.

data, although the distinctions made by Bernstein between 'elaborated' and 'restricted' codes (1961a) implied the potential fruitfulness of examining such answers and indicated some categories for analysis. One of the objectives of the Sociological Research Unit is to specify, if possible, the familial communication structure likely to be causally associated with differences in the subsequent language of the children, and variations in handling children's questions are likely to be an important determinant.

In earlier chapters we have been concerned with the more general problem of classifying and analysing answers to questions, anchoring the scheme where possible to Halliday's Scale and Category Grammar (Halliday, McIntosh and Strevens, 1964). This was pursued for structures at or below the unit of sentence and at the level of grammar. Lexical, contextual and mode levels were added, and, to increase the delicacy of the description of any answer, distinctions were made between appropriateness, completeness and the amount of presupposition of the answer. An answer to a 'who' question requires a nominal group for it to be grammatically appropriate, a nominal group which refers to a person to be lexically appropriate, and for contextual appropriateness and minimal contextual presupposition this lexical unit should refer unequivocally to the relevant person or persons. The use of a pronoun rather than a noun would involve contextual presupposition (realized as lexical incompleteness). A distinction between modes was made because the speaker sometimes has discretion in his choice of answer, viz. with 'why' questions a causal or consequence answer might be equally appropriate, or with 'who', a role specification or a proper name. This system was linked to Bernstein's distinction between 'restricted' and 'elaborated' codes (Chapter 4), but additional features of the mothers' answering tactics are also relevant to Bernstein's thesis, and these need to be mentioned and discussed before the specific predictions are expounded.

Four further features are examined here: whether questions are answered, the accuracy of the answers, the amount of information in the answers and the linguistic context in which the answers are embedded. The last two present difficulties. The amount of information is not easily measured. The total amount of speech to the child is one indirect index, but a more direct and probably more useful index can be obtained where answers can be broken up into discrete units of knowledge (objects, events or processes) which can be counted. A more hazardous venture is to count signs of vagueness and indefiniteness (lexical incompleteness) where greater precision is conventionally required and readily available.

The justification for examining the linguistic context of the answer is not easily or satisfactorily given, but the general question concerns the ease with which the child can extract knowledge about the physical and social world. The mother's utterance may be fragmented and unorganized, so that the child has to discard or rearrange sections of it. It may contain items not germane to the facts required by the question: 'noisy' items can be inserted which add no substantial information to the message, or items may be included for social-psychological reasons to indicate difference of status, to bias the listener's interpretation or to check upon his agreement. Such features may decrease the likelihood of the child receiving information directly relevant to the question posed.

If Bernstein's (1961a) thesis is correct, under appropriate conditions (and this setting should constitute such a situation), elaborated-code users should:

(1) Evade fewer questions.
(2) Give more accurate answers.
(3) Give more information in their answers.
(4) Show less disorganization in their answers.
(5) Have fewer 'noisy' items.
(6) Use fewer social psychological checks.
(7) For modes of answer to 'why' questions, they should prefer categorizations raised to a higher level of generality, arguments from analogy, causal and consequence explanations, and they should avoid denials of oddity, repetitions of questions as statements, appeals to authority or simple regularity and appeals to essence.

Simplified exemplars of these and the other categories for 'Why do leaves fall off the trees?' would be:

(1) Denial of oddity: Why shouldn't they?
(2) Repetition of question as statement: Because they do.
(3) Appeal to regularity: They fall every year.
(4) Appeal to essence: Leaves are like that.
(5) Appeal to authority: (Because it's the law).*
(6) Appeal to emotions and wishes: (Because I want to).*
(7) Explanation by analogy: The tree falls asleep and . . .
(8) Categorization: Leaves are alive and all living things die.
(9) Causal explanation: The strong winds of autumn blow them off.
(10) Consequence explanation: So that new leaves can come in the spring.

* These categories commonly appear for social or moral rather than physical problems.

It is suggested that middle-class mothers have an elaborated code available and will use it in this situation, but that the working-class mothers will generally be confined to a restricted code, although the situation ideally requires an elaborated one. If there are social-class differences similar to those suggested above, they should be one of the linking factors between the codes of the mother and her child.

2 Method

Subjects

The subjects comprised the mothers of 110 children of the factorial design subsampled from the original population (Chapter 5). This factorial sample had a two-way division on sex, social class and communication index and a three-way division on verbal intelligence test scores; there were five children in each cell. Since there were no low-I.Q., low-communication-index middle-class children, their 10 working-class equivalents were also dropped from this analysis. The imbalance resulted in an absence of low-I.Q. children, but this was unavoidable. The low-I.Q. children were not used for the analyses of variance or for the data reported in Table 6. 3: only the 80 high- and medium-I.Q. children were used for these (see Brandis and Henderson, 1970, for a comprehensive description).

Materials

The following questions were asked of the mother towards the end of the interview. Some interviewers did not use the phrases marked by brackets, and no mother answered the questions at the general level. The questionnaire contained an instruction that 'the layout is very formal, but it is at your discretion to move away from it when the mother has got the idea'. The interviewer said, 'I wonder if we could talk a little about everyday questions children often ask. What do you think you might say if X asked one of these?'

(1) (Children sometimes ask) why people have to do things. (Imagine X asking) Why does Daddy shave every morning? (What would you say?) The words in brackets are repeated for each question.
(2) . . . how things work . . . Where does the water in the tap come from? . . .
(3) . . . why things happen . . . Why do leaves fall off the trees? . . .
(4) . . . why people act as they do . . . Why did Mrs Jones cry when Johnny went into hospital? . . . .

(5) ... where things go or come from ... Where do I come from? ...
(6) ... who people are ... Who is the man who brings the milk? ...
(7) ... why they have to do things ... Why do I have to go to school in September? ...

Coding frame for answers

The examples to be given cover only the main differences noted. A full description of the scoring policy would be too lengthy and information is restricted to a minimum. Multiple coding was allowed.

One general problem was the desirability of separating speech to interviewer and speech to child. The answers the child would actually receive were only rarely given and mostly answers were in the form of reported speech. It may well be that the direct speech offered to the interviewer provides a better index of *how* the mother would convey the answer to the child than the reported speech to the child, although this is only a weak suggestion. Its putative similarity to the likely speech to the child lies in its direct rather than reported form, but other sociolinguistic features are different, e.g. age, extent of knowledge about the listener, nature of affective and authority relation to listener. The separation was not easy to achieve much of the time, especially for the linguistic features mentioned under (4) 'Context' (see below), but was maintained when possible and relevant. For the content of the answers the distinction was not necessary.

Answers were analysed under a series of headings:

(a) TACTICAL APPROACH TO QUESTIONS

A number of considerations are pertinent to the general orientation of the mother: whether the question is answered at all, the accuracy of the answer, the amount of information in the answer, and the linguistic context of the reply. Not all aspects were examined for all questions.

1 *Answer with no content for the child* Seven varieties of answer were scored which contained no speech that gave the child any information about the facts or beliefs questioned: (1) Explicit refusal to answer, (2) admission of not knowing what to say, (3) Admission of not knowing the answer, (4) Suggestion that the child refer the question to someone else, (5) Answer refused because the child is too young to understand, (6) Answer deferred until the child is older, (7) Unelaborated statements like 'I'd tell him' or 'I'd explain'.

2   *Accuracy of answer*   (*a*) *Untruths*

This was only scored for the question about the origin of babies. Only very rarely were other answers clearly wrong. The following answers were classified as inaccurate: (1) God, (2) baby bought or picked up, (3) gooseberry bush and variants. Sometimes God was cited as the paternal instigator of the process, although the remainder of the story was biologically correct. These were still scored as containing an inaccurate element. Although this may seem theoretically odd, the incidence of this addition was higher in the middle-class, and its inclusion as an error therefore reduces the probability of obtaining the predicted result that the working-class mothers should be less accurate overall.

(*b*) *Over-generalization*

'All', 'always', 'never', 'anything', 'everybody' can be used inaccurately to give features of the physical or social world a definiteness or universality which it does not have. When such words were judged to be misleading and 'most' or 'often' would have been better, they were classified as over-generalizations. Such a statement as 'All children go to school at five' was not scored in this way because this is very nearly true, so that the errors in scoring here might be considered biased in the direction of under-scoring.

3   *Amount of information in the answer*   (*a*) *Items of information*

The answers to the 'why' questions were not easily broken up into units of knowledge, but Questions 2 and, to a lesser extent, 5 were. For the origins of water in the tap three processes were counted: (1) pumping, (2) storage, and (3) purification, and five installations: (1) original source (sea, river, lake), (2) reservoir, (3) pumping station or waterworks, (4) pipes (four sets distinguished), and (5) tank in the house. In Question 5 six features were noted (1) seed/egg, (2) paternal role, (3) locus in mother, (4) baby's development, (5) baby's readiness to come out, and (6) baby's arrival.

(*b*) *Total number of words*

The total number of words spoken to the child by the mother is probably correlated with the amount of information proffered, and, since it was also necessary to have such a word count as a potential control for the assessment of the relative incidence of other linguistic features, this count was made.

H

(c) *Tokens of vagueness* (nouns and verbs)

In the nominal group 'thing' or 'something' can be used as uninformative substitutes for more precise heads, and 'do' or 'go' can perform a similar role in the verbal group. Only when it was judged that a more informative substitute should have been readily available was this category scored.

(d) *Indefinites*

All otherwise unqualified compound words with an initial morphemic 'some-' (except 'something') were labelled indefinite.

Both 3c and 3d are instances of lexical incompleteness, whereas 3d may be all that can be achieved as further information would not generally be available. As scored, items in 3c are unlikely to have occurred for this reason.

4 *Linguistic context of answers*   (a) *Substitutions and fragments*

A linguistic unit at or below the rank of sentence which is begun, but not completed, is called a fragment. If a rejected completed unit is replaced by a functionally similar one, it is a substitution. Here both were scored together.

(b) *Omissions*

Grammatical inappropriateness was the major cue for omissions, but occasionally semantic criteria had also to be applied.

While the over-generalizations (2b), tokens of vagueness (3c), and indefinites (3b) involve substitutions of contextually inappropriate or lexically incomplete structures, other features, bearing at least a family resemblance to them, appear to be additions to the core utterance. While the root meanings of such elements have informative meanings, they are frequently not used to convey these.

(c) *Tokens of vagueness* (adverbs and modifiers)

'Sort of', 'kind of', 'like' and 'more or less' can be added to nominal or verbal groups, not so much to attenuate the definiteness of these groups, but for other reasons as yet unknown.

(d) *Uninformative adjuncts*

'Actually' and 'really' can lose their emphatic function and unless this role was explicit, they were deemed uninformative.

(e) Redundant finishers

Used at the end of an utterance, 'and all that', 'sort of', and 'like' are often similar to 4c and d.

(f) Inessential phrases

'I mean', 'as a matter of fact', 'after all', and idiosyncratic variants identified by their repetition by an individual seem similar to 4e, but can occur at various junctures in an utterance.

(g) Simplifying adjuncts

Different from the preceding four are such words as 'just' and 'simply', in that these express a limitation upon the amount of speech likely to be given.

(h) Minimizers

It was noticed during preliminary perusals of scripts that some mothers made efforts to minimize the possible gravity of Johnny's departure for hospital (Q.4). These features were counted. Typical examples are 'he'll be better soon' and 'he's not very well', while the most extreme instance was a suggestion that mother's tears were provoked by her gladness that Johnny would soon be better.

(i) Tokens of uncertainty

'I think', 'perhaps', and 'probably' qualify utterances in a different way from earlier categories, implying reservations due to the complexity of the situation or a willingness to concede unsureness.

(j) Mirror images

Utterances can be concluded by inverted negated structures making a question: 'isn't it?', 'doesn't it?'

(k) Sympathetic circularity

Originally classified by Bernstein (1962b) with mirror images, 'you know' and 'you see' were separately scored, since they may have distinguishable functions.

Each of the foregoing categories was scored separately for speech to interviewer and speech to child, and the results are reported separately where possible. In cases of doubt, the policy was to score against the expected direction of differences.

(b) 'WHY' QUESTIONS

For the 'why' questions the ten varieties of modes mentioned in the Introduction were scored, but more delicate analyses were pursued within each mode.

Subdivisions within modes are given by questions:

Question 1 Four subcategories of purpose were used: (a) immediate purpose only (shaving off hairs), (b) social value (to look clean, smart), (c) personal wish, but of a third party, (d) physical value (to feel nice).

Question 3 Causal explanations were subdivided into (a) simple minimal (the leaves die, so they fall off), and (b) extended (the sap goes down, etc.).

Question 4 Direct appeals to emotion or wishes were divided upon three bases: (a) sadness, (b) worry, (c) not wanting child to go. Causal explanations were divided into (a) self-centred reasons (mother's loneliness) and (b) child-centred reasons (child's suffering).

Question 7 A division was made in category 8 between mothers who said that (a) all children had to go to school, and those who were more specific (b) that all five-year-old children had to go. Seven consequences were distinguished: (a) learning, with a count of the number of academic skills mentioned, (b) benefits of friendship, (c) avoidance of loneliness, (d) potential fun, (e) long-term goal—specific (to get a good job), (f) long-term goal—general (to be useful when you grow up), (g) appeal to identification (to be like your sister, father, etc.).

All scripts were coded by the two authors who had established a general agreement of 85 per cent on the 'why' questions and a higher incidence for the other categories, which were less ambiguous.

Treatment of results

A four-way comparison was made when desirable and necessary, contrasting social class, intelligence test scores, sex and communication index. The basic strategy was to compare with x^2 tests the relative proportions of mothers in opposed groups who used a particular category of answer, but when summed scores approximated to higher-order scales, analyses of variance were made. Results are presented in the following order: (A) Differences of tactics with the questions: (1) no answer to child, (2) accuracy of answer, (3) amount of information, (4) linguistic context of answer; (B) differences in modes of explanation for individual 'why' questions; (C) differences in modes of explanation for summed answers to all 'why' questions.

3   Results

A preliminary examination of the transcripts suggested there was insufficient variation in replies to Question 6 (Who is the man who brings the milk?) for systematic comparisons to be worthwhile. An examination of the initial tabulations showed that the communication index was irrelevant. Sex and I.Q. differences were generally small and insignificant, and to reduce the number of individual results reported comparisons yielding no significant differences are either ignored or only mentioned briefly.

(i) Variations in tactical approach to questions
(a) ANSWERS WITH NO CONTENT FOR THE CHILD

The incidence of the single categories was too low for individual comparisons; the distributions and content of the items made it sensible to collapse categories 1–6 as a 'minimal information' answer. There were reservations about incorporating 'referral to a third person (4)', but even if the preferred inference that referral decreased the chance of a child receiving an answer, is not justified, it remains true that the child is receiving no immediately informative reply. Concessions to the present limitation of the child's understanding (5 and 6) also reduced the amount of information available and sometimes appeared to be a socially acceptable means of hiding ignorance or unwillingness to answer. 'I'd tell him' of category 7 was treated separately, because there were no *a priori* reasons for assuming that this was an avoidance strategy.

Categories 1–6 were used at least once by only three middle, but thirteen working-class mothers of boys; for girls the numbers were four and thirteen. Both differences are significant (boys: $x^2 = 8.04$, $p < 0.01$; girls: $x^2 = 4.42$, $p < 0.05$). Use of category 7 alone showed a similar class bias (boys: $x^2 = 5.46$, $p < 0.05$; girls: $x^2 = 2.30$, $p < 0.01$), which is consistent with the possibility that it was an avoidance strategy. These answers were not evenly distributed across categories 1–6, 37 per cent were to Question 5, 'Where do I come from?' and 40 per cent to Question 2, 'Where does the water in the tap come from?'

(b) ACCURACY OF ANSWER

1 *Untruths* 'Where do I come from?' was the only question evoking sufficient inaccuracy to make scoring worthwhile. Working-class mothers of boys ($x^2 = 8 \cdot 67$, $p < 0 \cdot 01$) and, to a lesser extent, girls ($x^2 = 2 \cdot 19$, $p < 0 \cdot 1$) were more likely to avoid answering the question. Only one middle-class boy's mother failed to answer the question. Most of the working-class preference for 'I'd tell him', with no further explication, occurred to this question, but the significant difference remained without its inclusion. Of those giving answers which could be coded further, working-class mothers of boys were more likely to include untrue elements (God, gooseberry bushes, purchase) in their answers (boys: $x^2 = 5 \cdot 37$. $p < 0 \cdot 05$).

2 *Over-generalization* Across all questions there were no differences in the proportions of mothers using over-generalizations, but the incidence of this category was rather low (eight boys' mothers and seven girls' mothers).

(c) AMOUNT OF INFORMATION IN THE ANSWER

(1) The answers to the two 'where from?' questions were both divided into units of information. For Question 2 a significantly higher proportion of working- than middle-class mothers of both boys and girls did not give an answer codable in the specific frame. Of those who did, working-class boys' mothers were less likely to mention two or more types of 'installation' ($x^2 = 7 \cdot 82$, $p < 0 \cdot 01$), but not less likely to refer to 'processes'. For girls the results were in the same direction, but the level of the significances were reversed (mention of a process, $x^2 = 6 \cdot 30$, $p < 0 \cdot 05$; two or more types of installation: $x^2 = 2 \cdot 64$, $p < 0 \cdot 1$). An incidental finding was that the middle-class mothers of girls were relatively more likely to use a higher proportion of 'backward' explanations, from sink to sea ($x^2 = 10 \cdot 00$, $p < 0 \cdot 01$).

Similar results occurred with Question 5 about the origin of babies, after the 'no answer' and 'inaccurate answer' mothers had been eliminated. For boys whose mothers referred to the correct biological story the middle class mentioned more stages of development: seven out of twenty-three mentioned three or more stages, while only one working-class mother out of eight did so. Seven of the seventeen middle-class mothers who mentioned only one stage explicitly stated that their sons already knew the answer, while only one working-class mother claimed this. Unfortunately, numbers had so diminished by this third stage that statistical comparisons were likely to be unreliable. For girls there were no class differences.

2 *Number of words* Table 6.1 shows the mean number of words addressed by mothers of boys and girls to the interviewer and to the child for all six questions analysed. Analyses of variance (Table 6.2) showed that it was only for the speech addressed to boys that social class and I.Q. have relevance: middle-class, high-I.Q. boys received twice as many words as working-class, medium-I.Q. boys. I.Q. was significant, but social class was not. This is because of the large variance. Some mothers produced answers of 300 words to a single question (this was almost always to the interviewer and usually for the question about the origin of babies). The longest 5 per cent of answers were all reduced to a score of eighty words to avoid single responses unduly biasing the means. The girls' means for speech to interviewer look different, but again the variances were so high that none were significantly so (Table 6.1).

TABLE 6.1 *Mean number of words addressed by mothers to interviewer and child for children of different sex, I.Q. and social class*

		Boys				Girls		
	n	*No. words to interviewer*	*No. answers reduced to 80*	*No. of words to child*	*n*	*No. words to interviewer*	*No. answers reduced to 80*	*No. of words to child*
Middle class, high I.Q.	10	99	3	189	10	60	1	105
Middle class, medium I.Q.	10	90	3	104	10	127	4	117
Working class, high I.Q.	10	88	4	131	10	106	2	113
Working class, medium I.Q.	10	105	2	91	10	118	5	96

TABLE 6.2 *Number of words addressed to boys by mother as a function of I.Q. and social-class (n = 40)*

Source of variation	df	Variance estimate	F ratio	p value
I.Q. (high>medium)	1	38,751	12·23	<0·01
Social class (middle>working)	1	12,426	3·92	<0·1
Interaction I.Q. × Social class	1	4,906	1·55	—
Within groups	36	3,169	—	—

Although there was considerable intersubject variability in the amount of speech, and some of this could be attributed to the independent variables, no controls for length of utterance were made: most analyses were confined to dividing mothers into users and non-users of categories of speech and the reduction of scores to proportions would not have affected such classifications (see Table 6.3).

3 and 4 *Vagueness and indefiniteness* Neither the nominal or verbal group tokens of vagueness nor indefinites (Table 6.3) were differentially distributed by the variables examined here.

(d) LINGUISTIC CONTEXT OF ANSWERS

Social class was the only variable differentially associated with the eleven variables examined under this heading and, in all but one case of a significant difference, it was the working-class mothers who were more likely to use such structures (see Table 6.3).

The middle-class mothers of boys were more likely to minimize the gravity of the hospital entry. While there was no evidence to support the view that the working class were more likely to *substitute* indefinite words or tokens of vagueness, there were several signs of a greater propensity to *add* a variety of structures. These comprised uninformative adjuncts, redundant finishers, and simplifying adjuncts, while inessential phrases almost achieved significance for girls. These differences were obtained in spite of the greater number of words generally addressed by middle-class mothers of boys to the interviewer.

Sympathetic circularity attained significance only for the girls, but the direction of the difference for boys was the same.

(ii) Individual 'why' questions

The distributions in Table 6.4 show the percentages of categories used. A single maternal answer could contain several categories and the apparent variability is misleading. The number of types of answer per question was small, and the non-modal responses were too rare to provide differentiation. For three of the four questions no variable was associated with a significant difference in the use of modes, although directional trends were never opposed to expectation. Question 7, 'Why do I have to go to school in September?' evoked the most replies and the most varied replies, and for this question differences began to attain significance. For boys, the middle class were slightly less likely to confine a consequence

TABLE 6.3 *Numbers of middle- and working-class mothers using structures relevant to the amount of information or its linguistic context*

Variable	Addressee	Boys Middle class	Working class	x^2	Girls Middle class	Working class	x^2
2 Amount of information:							
2c Vagueness (noun and verb)	Child	12	9		9	5	
	Interviewer	9	6		9	8	
d Indefinites	Both	4	5		3	4	
4 Linguistic context							
4a Fragments and substitutions	Child	7	7		9	8	
b Omission	Child	8	12		9	10	
c Vagueness (advbs. and modifiers)	Child	1	2		2	1	
	Interviewer	5	5		4	5	
d Uninformative adjuncts	Both	2	9	4·51*	6	8	
e Redundant finishers	Child	0	7	6·23*	4	12	5·10*
	Interviewer	1	10	8·03†	2	5	
	Both	1	12	11·40†	4	13	6·55*
f Inessential phrases	Both	2	6		2	8	3·33
g Simplifying adjuncts	Both	5	9		6	15	6·42*
h Minimizers	Child	14	3	10·23†	7	7	
i Tokens of uncertainty:							
Verb	Both	12	12		10	11	
Adjuncts	Both	6	5		4	5	
j Mirror images	Both	2	4		3	4	
k Sympathetic circularity	Both	6	11		6	15	6·42*
n		20	20		20	20	

* Means $p < 0.05$; † means $p < 0.01$.

answer to a single reason (10a: commonly 'to learn') ($x^2 = 2.66$, $p < 0.1$), were more likely to mention a precise age (8b: because you are five) ($x^2 = 4.50$, $p < 0.05$), and invoke rules (5: because it's the law) ($x^2 = 4.88$, $p < 0.05$). Only one case of (5) without (8) occurred in the middle class. Girls showed no differences.

TABLE 6.4 *Percentage distributions of modes of answers to 'why' questions*

Mode		All questions 1, 3, 4, 7	1 shaving	3 leaves	4 hospital	7 school
3a	Regularity	2·3	3·7	28·0		
b		10·5	4·5			4·1
4	Essence	1·1	0·7	3·7		
5	Appeal to authority					4·1
6	Direct appeal to emotions	1·4			(68·0)	
6a		13·5	0·7		51·2	
6bc					16·8	
7	Analogy	3·8		14·7		
8	Categorization	7·7	9·0	1·2		16·1
8a						
8b						
9	Causal	13·5	5·2	(21·5)	(32·0)	1·8
9a				16·6	23·2	
b				4·9	8·8	
10	Consequence	46·3	(76·2)	20·9		(73·7)
10a			46·3			49·3
b			18·7			1·8
c			7·5			0·5
d			3·7			4·6
e						4·1
f						8·3
g						5·1
n		639	134	163	125	217

(iii) Differences in the use of modes of explanation over all 'why' questions

Middle-class mothers of boys used fewer repetitions of questions as statements (2) (boys: $x^2 = 8·88$, $p < 0·01$), but this was linked to the child's verbal I.Q. (boys: $x^2 = 5·37$, $p < 0·05$). There were tendencies for middle-class mothers to employ analogies (7) (boys: $x^2 = 0·83$, girls: $x^2 = 3·09$, $p < 0·10$: for sexes combined: $x^2 = 4·08$, $p < 0·05$) and a weaker one for them to avoid statements of regularity alone (3a) (boys: $x^2 = 1·86$, $p < 0·1$; for the sexes combined $x^2 = 2·69$, $p < 0·1$).

Two final analyses contrasted the social class and I.Q. groups for the total number of appeals to consequence (10) and the total number of other 'acceptable' reasons (5–9). Analyses of variance showed that the middle-class mothers of girls and boys gave significantly more 'acceptable' reasons in all (5–9) than the working class, but the difference was not significant for appeals to consequence alone.

Interactions of class and I.Q. were significant for total explanations (5–9), but once more not quite so for appeals to consequence alone (Tables 6.5 and 6.6). Mothers of high-I.Q. boys gave more 'acceptable' reasons in total than mothers of medium-I.Q. boys.

TABLE 6.5 (i) *Variations in total number of 'acceptable' (categories 5–9*) reasons by social-class and intelligence-test scores: boys*

Source of variance	df	Variance estimate	F ratio	p
Social class (middle>working)	1	10·0	8·31	<0·01
I.Q. (high>medium)	1	4·9	4·07	<0·05
Interaction: class × I.Q.	1	10·0	8·31	<0·01
Residual	36	43·3		

TABLE 6.5 (ii) *Variations in total number of 'acceptable' (categories 5–9*) reasons by social-class and intelligence-test scores: girls*

Source of variance	df	Variance estimate	F ratio	p
Social class (middle>working)	1	16·9	8·95	<0·01
I.Q. (high>medium)	1	0·8	0·42	
Interaction: class × I.Q.	1	8·1	4·28	<0·05
Residual	36	68·0		

* 3 was counted if the appeal to regularity was qualified

TABLE 6.6 *Variations in total number of consequence (category 10) reasons by social-class and intelligence-test scores: boys*

Source of variance	df	Variance estimate	F ratio	p
Social class (middle>working)	1	7·2	2·39	<0·2
I.Q. (high>medium)	1	0·9	0·30	
Interaction: class × I.Q.	1	10·9	3·62	<0·1
Residual	36	108·4		

4 Discussion

Six predictions made upon the basis of Bernstein's theoretical position were supported by the results: middle-class mothers differed
from working-class mothers in that they evaded fewer questions,
gave more accurate answers, gave more information in their answers,
used fewer 'noisy' items, used fewer social psychological checks on
agreement and preferred certain modes of answering 'why' questions.
A seventh, that their answers should be less disorganized, was not
supported.

The indices of disorganization, fragments and substitutions have
not as yet been shown to have any empirical validity and their total
incidence in the speech analysed here was low. 78 per cent of the
mothers used at least one fragment or substitution, but it had been
expected that there would be many more of these examples of non-
fluency in the mothers' speech and that the analysis would be of
differences between means rather than a Yes/No dichotomy. The
relative fluency of the mothers' speech suggests that this task was not
difficult for them. If this was so, then the failure to find class differences may not be surprising. Bernstein (1962a) has argued and
shown that working-class adolescent boys should be and are more
fluent than their peers in that they use a longer phrase length and a
shorter mean pause duration, but at the same time they also use
words of shorter length. A linguistic analysis of the same data
(Bernstein, 1962b) showed grammatical and lexical class differences
consistent with the expectation that the middle-class subjects were
using an elaborated code, but the working-class a restricted one. It
would only be under conditions where the restricted-code user felt
constrained to try to use an elaborated code at a level beyond his
present competence that his speech should become more disorganized.
Hence both the existence of group differences and its direction will
be a function of the level of coding attempted. This situation does
not appear to have forced the working-class mothers to move
towards use of an elaborated code too difficult for them, with a
consequent breakdown in fluency.

Differences between boys and girls were slight, except for the total
amount of speech addressed to the child. Although I.Q. was the only
significant source of variation for the boys, partly because within
groups variances were so high, it would seem safe to infer that high-
I.Q. middle-class boys are likely to receive special treatment: on
average 75 per cent more speech than the other groups. This is consistent with the finding that the total number of adequate reasons
given in answer to 'why' questions is linked to both I.Q. and social

class for boys only, although class and the class/I.Q. interaction were significant for girls and the other differences and similarities between the social classes do not vary systematically between boys and girls.

I.Q. was of little relevance except in relation to the two measures of quantity of output mentioned above, and with these it remains unknown whether the variance is a result of brighter boys demanding more speech from the mothers, brighter mothers having brighter sons and talking to them more, or high quantities of maternal speech enhancing verbal I.Q.

The failure of the communication index to differentiate between the answers of mothers is disappointing. This is consistent with its irrelevance to children's answers to questions (Chapter 5), but inconsistent both with its constituent items, concerned as they are with responses to questions, and its correlation with attitude to toys. In this case (Bernstein and Young, 1967) it had an effect additive to social class, although itself positively correlated with class. It has played a similar role in analyses of lexical usage by children (Brandis and Henderson, 1970).

Social class, however, successfully differentiated across the whole range of variables studied, and this was in spite of the several limitations of design and data control. There were only six answers available for analysis, a small sample. For the four 'why' questions the actual question was a major determinant of the mode of answer leaving little opportunity for variation to occur: 76 per cent of answers to why Daddy shaves were purposive, 59 per cent of answers to why leaves fall were appeals to regularity or consequence, 68 per cent of answers to why Mother cried when her Johnny was taken were appeals to emotion, and 74 per cent of reasons for having to go to school were appeals to consequence. To gain a comprehensive picture of social-class differences in mode preference, it would be necessary to increase the number of questions and select these so that there was greater variability of response to account for.

This lack of variation is relevant to two other areas examined. Once it had been shown that the middle-class mothers were more likely to answer Questions 2 and 5, there was only a rump working-class sample left to examine the types and amount of information. Fortunately, just sufficient remained to answer these questions. The second area was the linguistic measures of accuracy, amount and context of information. For many categories the incidence of the categories was too low for reasonable comparison (over-generalization (2b), indefinites (3d), vagueness of adverbs and modifiers (4c), inessential phrases (4f), tokens of uncertainty, adjuncts (4i) and mirror images (4j)).

This was particularly unfortunate, because the construction of a matrix of some measures of association (Φ coefficients) of these variables could have led to clarification of the most suitable principles upon which to classify them. An uncompleted analysis of the possible reasons for using these features and their effects upon the listener shows that there is potentially considerable overlap in their causes and consequences, which only an empirical analysis can illuminate. For example, a highly general word like 'thing' might be used because it is the most appropriate available or because the speaker is unable or unwilling to select a more precise token. This contrast between generality and unnecessary vagueness or indefiniteness applies to many other items scored. It would be expected that the mother with an elaborated code will favour more general explanations when desirable, whereas the restricted-code mother will have difficulty selecting more appropriate words than 'thing' quickly. If this argument is valid, there are pressures encouraging both types of code user to use 'thing' and a single unprobed situation cannot be used to differentiate between them. More control over the empirical situation is required to test the implications of this argument.

It would appear that in the situation studied here the working-class are not *substituting* more vague or indefinite words, but that they are *adding* features (uninformative adjuncts, redundant finishers, simplifying adjuncts and inessential phrases). It is, however, possible that at an earlier point in time they had this function, but that their incidence has been extended, so that they are now scattered at points where coding difficulty might occur. Sometimes they are functional for the speaker, but much of the time they do not seem to be so. Listening to people conversing, one can notice the frequent occurrence of such items apparently having no value. The speaker may not even be aware of their presence, so far have they penetrated his idiolect. Certain words and phrases are idiosyncratic, but others characterize social groups or the whole language culture. There is probably social pressure to reduce the incidence of these items, particularly in the middle class. It might therefore be suggested that the working class are more likely to retain them. To use Allport's phrase, such features have possibly developed into functionally autonomous habits, but at the same time retain their potential as pause-fillers. This could be demonstrated by showing that people have a 'normal' rate of producing such features, which can be increased by raising the level of difficulty of the task, as Goldman-Eisler (1961) showed for pauses.

This should be true regardless of class, but the particular features might not be the same for both classes. For example, tokens of uncertainty might increase more for the middle class. The investigation of these words requires integration with work on unfilled pauses, repetitions, fragments and substitutions and articulation rates to form a unified field of study, and such partial studies as this one can only provide factual information for subsequent explanation.

The analysis of the 'why' questions also suffered from paucity of data, but the results were generally in line with expectation and testify to the validity of the predictions made. This line of inquiry is pursued for children with a greater variety of questions (Chapter 7) and where stronger support for the hypotheses least adequately tested here is given.

While several studies (Bernstein, 1962a and 1962b; Lawton, 1963 and 1964; Robinson, 1965a and 1965b; Robinson and Creed, 1968; Hawkins, 1969) have shown social-class differences in the speech and writing of children and adolescents in free and structured contexts, this study extends these differences to adults and in particular to a primary socializing agent.

This study differs from the others referred to in that here the mother reported to an interviewer what she *would* say to her child, and the problem of validity arises more strongly. Would mothers, in fact, say what they report they would say? No external check on maternal behaviour was available.

Direct observation with the child actually asking the question would have still involved the presence of an interviewer, while the collection of naturally occurring questions would have raised technological difficulties of considerable proportions and, if resolved, would have still left a lack of comparability of questions.

To standardize the questions and render the study administratively viable, some compromise on potential validity like the one taken was necessary. One major worry is that the middle-class mothers are more likely to have given socially desirable answers than working-class mothers, and this could have led to an over-estimation of the child's opportunities for learning from his questions. A second worry is that the interview situation may have been more stressful and disruptive for working- than middle-class mothers. Neither difficulty was overcome, but certain ameliorative observations can be made. Tape-recordings of the interviews gave no indication that the working- and middle-class mothers experienced differential stress. Neither did the interviewers report any. Similarly, there was no suggestion that the middle-class were actively contriving desirable responses. It should be remembered that the questions did not have a closed response set, where a socially desirable answer was overtly contrasted with other choices. Further, although child-rearing manuals may prescribe the desirability of answering questions and offer guidance about ways of dealing with awkward questions, they do not usually offer explicit specific tactics and strategy. That the middle-class are more likely to consult such manuals is probably indicative of their concern to do what is best rather than to have appropriate opinions available for interviews and conversations.

The direct evidence concerning the reliability and validity of the mothers' answers comes from the study of their seven-year-old children's answers to similar questions (Chapter 7). What are the relationships between mothers' and children's answers? If there is considerable correspondence and no alternative sources from which the children could have learned their answers, it is reasonable to cite the mother as the most likely source.

The inclination to believe such a story should be increased when an explanation of such a correspondence can be offered, and Bernstein's theory does provide this theoretical framework. An effective description of these connections is best made if a summary of results from another mother/child interaction situation is included.

Cook (1971) is examining the mothers' behaviour in discipline situations. Mothers were asked what they would do and say if their child would not go to school, wanted to watch TV instead of going to bed, and how she would behave in three other situations. A complicated coding frame was developed to categorize the responses, but three only are of immediate significance: non-verbal strategies, positional appeals and personal appeals. Imperative strategies include brief commands like 'Shut up!' as well as smacks and moving children forcibly. Positional appeals are general rules governing the behaviour of wide categories of people, e.g. 'Boys don't . . .', 'Only babies would . . .', whereas in personal appeals individuals are specified and the consequences of the misdemeanour can be made explicit, both in terms of overt behaviour and feelings associated with these, e.g. 'You won't have enough sleep and you'll feel tired and miserable tomorrow morning.' Although working- and middle-class mothers used equal numbers of positional appeals, the working-class made more frequent mention of imperative strategies and less frequent mention of personal appeals, particularly those directed at the child.

Before we ask what is made available for the child to learn, we may observe the differences in the medium of instruction. The middle-class are more likely to use language, the working-class imperative means. In the personal appeals, explanations are offered which link the misdemeanour to other events, backwards or forwards in time, and the experience of these events may be linked to associated emotional states. Information about both the physical and social world may be given in such a form as to encourage the child to make independent judgments in the future.

The working-class child receiving imperative demands will be receiving information of a different order. On a classical conditioning paradigm, all contiguous stimuli should become associated with the pain of punishment. At the best, as far as accurate communication is concerned, the child is left to infer the connection between his own behaviour and the mother's reactions. Not only may learning be more confused; there may be less in such situations.

With positional appeals, the child is being given a simple and often universal rule. He is being given appropriate rules of conduct for certain general roles. but with no ancillary explanation. If he successfully learns what five-year-olds should and should not do, it may not stand him in good stead when he gets older. Such knowledge will not be cumulative if it relates to age status. As one gets older one can test whether the rule still applies, but that is all. These abrupt role specifications may mark the beginnings of the alleged simple but rigid role structure found in the working-class, and, as Bernstein has suggested, language is used to define these role relationships.

(It would be interesting to know whether Piaget's (1932) propositions about the rigidity ascribed to rules by young children derives not so much from their conceptual limitations as from the positional appeals to which they are exposed. To ask 'Why?' in the face of a personal appeal is to ask for information, but to ask 'Why?' to a positional appeal is a challenge to authority—and a threat to the system. Perhaps children learn to accept universal prescriptions and have to unlearn them later.)

Cook's results accord with the Bernstein thesis both in the differential usage and function of language for the two social classes. What is learned is likely to be different.

Our results and Cook's are complementary. The 'wh' questions from the children should encourage mothers to *communicate* information about the world through the use of language to which the middle-class mothers duly conform. The working-class mothers more frequently treat the questions as *control* problems. Their non-answering ensures a minimal amount of information being transmitted, their restatements of the question and simple appeals to regularity and to tradition discourage further information-seeking questions, but at the same time assert maternal authority. Although the discipline situations might be expected to encourage the *control* which the working-class exercise, the middle-class show a tendency to treat the situations as opportunities to *communicate* facts about things and people.

In both cases the information conveyed via language to the working-class child has the same character—simple general rules.

I

These rules are isolated from each other and all at a single level of abstraction. You have to learn the list.

However, the middle-class is not only receiving more information; this information is organized. The answers to 'why' questions relate particular events to other events earlier in time (causes) and events later in time (consequences and functions). The arguments by analogy imply a building up of similarities across different topics. These co-ordinate relationships introduce associations across topics and may well attune the child to differences as well as similarities in the world. The use of category explanations introduces different levels of knowledge to the child. He can also build up super-ordinate and sub-ordinate relationships. Such a hierarchical system of knowledge and belief has a deductive potential not available to the working-class child. A new problem presented to a middle-class child is more likely to be seen as similar to other problems previously encountered, and the child is better placed to take decisions regarding such a problem by examining its relationship to his systematized knowledge and belief. This should apply to social and moral problems as well as those of the physical world. He has therefore a greater potential for becoming a self-organizing system, able to act independently—and language has been the vehicle by which this is accomplished. The working-class child, on the other hand, has to search for a rule that may fit.

Other differences are also relevant. The middle-class child is learning a different 'semantic' for 'why'. That his questions are answered may mean that he will find obtaining answers to questions a source of satisfaction and increase the probability of him asking further questions. There should be motivational consequences as well as cognitive results.

Whether there is evidence to support these ideas as far as the children themselves are concerned is taken up in the next chapter.

Chapter 7   Answers to 'wh' questions: seven-year-old children

1   Introduction

The initial encouragement from the preliminary analyses of the answers to 'wh' questions by five-year-old children (Chapter 5), further heightened by the discovery of theoretically consistent differences between working- and middle-class mothers in their ways of handling their children's questions (Chapter 6), naturally led us to pursue children's answers to 'wh' questions more thoroughly and systematically. We set out to describe more comprehensively the grammatical. lexical and semantic features of children's answers to a wide range of 'wh' questions (Chapters 2 and 3), and as far as possible the investigation to be reported here attempts to isolate social sources of variation in the use of such features of language, especially in so far as these can be united to Bernstein's theoretical framework (Chapter 4).

How far these objectives are realized is discussed at the end of the chapter, but the investigation is perhaps an instance of pride coming before a fall, or at least ambitious enthusiasm resulting in stomach upsets, depressions and intermittent tear-shedding and hair-tearing on the personal side and a less than definitive clarification of the answering behaviour of children on the scientific side. To anticipate the occasions of distress: we tried to answer too many questions at once, incorporating and hoping to isolate the differential relevance of too many independent variables with too few subjects in each sub-group, A sympathetic critic might say that we were too optimistic both about the magnitude of the differences to be found between sub-groups of children and the clarity of the pattern of such differences. We seriously under-estimated the complexities of the speech data obtained. The analyses reported in Chapters 5 and 6 required only a small number of scoring categories which could be quickly and reliably coded. But, as the contents of Chapters 2 and 3 have threatened and Appendix B (Vol. II) shows, the persistent application of a divergent intelligence can generate many divisions of possible usefulness. At one stage we were handling well over 100 scores per child, a number beyond our span of immediate comprehension.

One final complication was added to the experimental procedure which needs to be mentioned, although it produced no exciting results. We judged it worthwhile to probe initial answers that children gave to the 'why' questions asked of them. There was a two-fold reason behind this. According to our thinking, the middle-class child develops a more organized set of beliefs about his total environment than his working-class peer. For example, he comes to see objects and events as members of sets with co-ordinate and subordinate members and themselves members of super-ordinate categories, e.g. 'cat' is co-ordinate with 'dog', has sub-ordinate members, 'Persian', 'Abyssinian', 'tabby', and itself is a member of super-ordinate sets, e.g. 'mammals', 'four-legged creatures', 'domestic pets', etc. These sets can be arranged according to a variety of criteria dependent upon the attributes of immediate interest. This emphasizes both similarities and differences. It was expected that middle-class children would be more aware of more of these groupings, not only with respect to classificatory systems, but also to the temporal and causal dimensions; middle-class children should become more encouraged to see objects and events as having antecedent and subsequent states and stages, associated causally with each other.

Our probing of the children's answers to 'why' questions was intended to expose the network of associated knowledge and belief surrounding an event. If a child were to construe an experimental situation in which 'Why do the leaves fall off the trees?' were asked as one in which only a single-sentence answer is to be given, the experimenter could underestimate the complexity of the child's belief system. Similar considerations might apply to the working-class child for the same or different reasons: he might find that short, uninformative replies enable him to escape from a boring, sinister, embarrassing or stupid situation. It has been argued that social-class differences in speech are an artefact of the experimenter's failure to provide adequate opportunity for the working-class children to manifest their competence.

To avoid under-estimating or over-estimating the extent of the differences between sub-groups of children, we did try to give them a chance to expand upon their initial answers by giving them up to three further questions (probes) whose form and content were contingent upon the nature of the child's first and subsequent responses.

Because we made our experimental situation and our data-processing too complicated, what follows is not a true record of everything we did, although we hope that what we omit does not invalidate our interpretations, but only renders the presentation of the results clearer. Of course, as Medawar (1967) argues, there are considerable and necessary differences between what goes on in laboratories and what appears to have been done as far as the published report indicates, and hopefully we have not made any errors of judgment in excess of these desiderata.

But, to begin again at the beginning, when hopes were high that the investigation would yield a definitive description of aspects of answers to 'wh' questions in seven-year-olds. The goals of the investigation were:

1 To develop further and test empirically the taxonomic scheme for answers to questions described in Chapters 2 and 3, viz. to examine the usefulness of the ideas of appropriateness, completeness and presupposition at the levels of context, mode, grammar and lexis.

2 To specify social-class differences in the use of these linguistic categories and test their relationship to those which Bernstein's theoretical framework (Chapter 4) would enable us to predict.

3 To proceed in several ways beyond the notion of broadly contrasted 'social class' groupings as a basis for establishing differences by showing that:

(i) Participation in a 'Use of Language' programme (Gahagan and Gahagan, 1970) would make lower-working-class children's answers more like those of their middle-class peers than they might otherwise have been.

(ii) That differences in language usage at age five among working-class girls would be relevant to differences in answers to 'wh' questions at age seven.

(iii) That 'social class' would still be an operative variable for children living in a neighbourhood predominantly of a different social class. In particular, middle-class children in a mainly working-class borough would tend to answer questions like their social class rather than their neighbourhood peers.

(iv) That certain patterns of communication and control within the family would be effective predictors of answering behaviour in the family (Brandis and Henderson, 1970; Bernstein and Young, 1967).

4 To attempt to assess the relative significance of (1) social class, (2) control and communication index (see below) and (3) verbal intelligence test scores as independent associates of answering behaviour utilizing partial correlations.

Hypotheses

Although we can specify a number of predictions from Bernstein's theoretical statements, we hoped that detailed detective work at the data-coding stage would suggest other calculations worth making, consistent (or even inconsistent) with the theory.

Our general expectation was that our subsidiary independent variables, viz. participation in the 'Use of Language' programme, complexity of speech at age five and a high communication and control index would have similar effects to being middle class, but weaker.

Relative to their working-class peers, middle-class children should use:

(1) At the level of context, less contextual inappropriateness and incompleteness and less unjustified presupposition (revealed in choice of mode and in the selection of lexical terms unfamiliar to the listener).

(2) At the level of mode selection: (*a*) more objective modes of answering 'when' and 'where' questions, (*b*) in response to 'why' questions, more appeals to analogy, cause and consequence, but fewer denials of oddity, restatements of question as answer, appeals to essence, regularity or tradition; more appeals to categorization when these have explanatory value, but fewer when they do not. There should also be a lesser incidence of modes inappropriate to the content of the question and fewer irrelevant answers.

(3) At the formal level of grammar, less grammatical inappropriateness and incompleteness, but more presupposition—and probably more flexibility in language use indicated by grammatically acceptable substitutions and fewer grammatical mistakes.

(4) At the formal level of lexis, less lexical inappropriateness and incompleteness, and, if it should occur, more appropriate lexical substitution.

(5) Under probing into answers to 'why' questions, a more systematic hierarchy of knowledge and belief should be revealed, with retreats to repetitions and restatements being less common.

2 Method

Materials: selection of questions

Since the simplest response to a 'closed' question is a 'Yes' or 'No', and multiple-choice questions already provide the respondent with most of the linguistic form and all the content of a minimally acceptable reply, such questions were omitted and attention was focused upon the 'open' 'wh' questions. The actual questions included were evaluated against a number of criteria:

(1) Each of the 'wh' words, except 'which', should be represented, and 'how' questions should cover the first three of the four modes mentioned in Chapters 2 and 3: (1) verb ascriptive, e.g. 'How are you?', (2) verb non-ascriptive, e.g. 'How well do you read?', and (3) method, e.g. 'How do you build a cupboard?'

(2) The 'who', 'where' and 'when' questions should each be such that we might reasonably expect that the child would know the answer to the question, even though he might not be able to express this verbally. Three 'where' (Q.2, 4, 6), three 'when' (Q.1, 11, 18) and two 'who' (Q.9, 12) questions were included.

(3) The 'how' questions should also be within the capacity of the children to answer. Simple mode 1 was not included, but one requiring an intensive complement was (Q. 22). Mode 2 was represented by Q.8, Mode 3 by Q.7 and Q.15. Q.7, Q.24 and Q.30, were in fact incorporated at other people's request.

(4) Two 'what' questions (Q.5, 10) within the children's range of experience were selected.

(5) It was thought worthwhile to incorporate some compound interrogative markers, so two 'what for' (Q.3, 19) and two 'where from' (Q.17, 28) judged to be within the children's capacity were included.

(6) 'Why' questions were more problematical. We wished to include some questions originally posed to the mothers, for comparative purposes (not in fact realized), but the mothers' answers had already shown that some questions were more likely to evoke particular modes of response than others (p. 110), sometimes because of the form and context of the questions, but sometimes as a function of the subject-matter itself. A probably relevant distinction which quickly came to mind was between questions about physical—that is, empirical—matters and moral matters. We chose to include moral and natural science questions, but decided to add one human biological (Q.13) and one 'social' question (Q.21) originally posed to the mothers. We had to pose questions vaguely within the capacity of seven-year-old children, and after a brief reading of Piaget and Nathan Isaacs (1930) and an examination of the comprehension section of the Wechsler Intelligence Scale for Children (Wechsler, 1949), we elected for four moral (Q.14, 20, 26, 29) and four physical (Q.16, 23, 25, 27) questions.

(7) The time taken to interview the children should not exceed half an hour, and thirty questions seemed to give a reasonable compromise of expected duration and coverage.

To decide the order in which questions should be posed, a randomizing procedure was used with some constraints: e.g. Q.7 should come immediately after Q.6 and Q.24 after Q.23, and that the more difficult and searching 'why' questions should not be among the first ten asked. The only unfortunate result of this was the close proximity of the three 'where' questions (Q.2, 4, 6), which perhaps predisposed children to use answers already given as reference-points for the subsequent 'where' questions.

The complete questionnaire is given below.

The questions

In so far as words in questions are stressed, those underlined should carry it.

1 When do you go home from school?
2 Where is your home?
3 What is a home for?
4 Where does your best friend live?
5 What is a friend?
6 Where is your favourite sweet-shop?
7 How do you buy sweets?
8 How well can you read?
9 Who gives you lessons at school?
10 What is a school?
11 When did you start at Infant school?
12 Who is the man who sees you when you are ill?
13 Why are people sometimes ill? (2 probes.)
14 Why shouldn't you hit children smaller than yourself? (2 probes.)
15 Can you tell me how to ride a bicycle?
16 Why does wood float? (2 probes.)
17 Where does milk come from? (If child answers 'cows', ask Why?)
18 When was your birthday?
19 What are birthdays for?
20 Why shouldn't anyone tell lies? (2 probes.)
21 Why does Daddy shave every morning? (2 probes.)
22 How tall would you like to be when you are grown up?
23 Why do the leaves fall off the trees? (2 probes.)
24 How do the leaves fall off the trees?
25 Why does a ball come down when you throw it up in the air? (2 probes.)
26 Why shouldn't anyone steal? (2 probes.)
27 Why does the sea have waves? (2 probes.)

28 Where does the water in the tap come from?
29 Why should children do what their parents tell them to? (2 probes.)
30 Tell me all the different things you can do with a piece of string.

Instructions and procedure

An attempt was made to make the subjects feel at ease in a friendly, relaxed atmosphere. All the children had encountered the experimenters several times before. Girls were interviewed by a woman, boys by a man. Each subject was seen individually, and the child sat at a small table at right angles to the experimenter. Instructions were given slowly, clearly and quietly, and the child was given periodic encouragement by such remarks as 'You are answering nicely,' 'Lovely', although phrases implying that answers were correct were avoided.

When the child had sat down and greetings had been exchanged, the experimenter said:

'I've got all sorts of questions here about different things. There are quite a lot of them and they are just the sort of questions that children and other people sometimes ask. Some of them are interesting ones, some are a bit funny and some are ordinary ones. We are going to play a game with them. Let's see how you answer them. Let's start with something you do at home, like: "What do you like to eat for breakfast?" . . . . And now one about animals: "What are baby cats called?" . . . And here's a question that puzzles some people: "Why does it get dark at night?". . .' (If the child did not give an answer to this question, the experimenter said, 'Yes; that is a puzzling question, isn't it? You answered the others nicely. Now we'll do these!') If the child did attempt an answer, the experimenter said, 'You answered those three nicely. Now we'll do these.'
The questions given above were then asked.

Rarely for questions other than those introduced by 'why' the child did not give a useful answer, in which case the experimenter introduced a new question intended to be equivalent, e.g. 'Where is your favourite sweet-shop?' 'I don't have a favourite.' 'But you do buy sweets?' 'Yes' 'Where is one shop where you buy sweets?'
Answers to 'why' questions were probed. The original intention was to explore the framework of belief associated with the explanation offered, e.g.: Q. 'Why are people sometimes ill?' R. 'They get germs.' Probe: 'Why do they get germs?' The simple instruction to

the experimenters to use the first answer as a focus for the next question proved unworkable in practice. Experimenters were therefore given discretion to ask such questions as, for example, 'Is there any other reason why people are sometimes ill?', so that the probing technique was not as uniform as we would have liked. The variations arose for several reasons, but one over which experimenters had no control was that the modes used for the first response themselves constrained the type of probe possible.

Independent variables

The index of social class has been described in Chapter 5. The intelligence test scores used here were English Picture Vocabulary Test scores (Brimer and Dunn, 1962). This leaves three variables undefined: the 'Use of Language' programme, speech complexity and the control and communication index.

The *'Use of Language' programme* is described in detail in another monograph in this series (Gahagan and Gahagan, 1970). Suffice it to say here that the essential purpose of the programme was to switch children whose life-chances predicted confinement to a restricted code on to the elaborated code functions and structures of the language. For twenty minutes a day the class teachers worked through a variety of games and tasks intended to achieve this end. The programme had been running five terms when our investigation took place. There is little obvious connection between any activity in the programme and answering 'wh' questions, and hence direct positive transfer is improbable. If the 'Use of Language' programme children do differ from their controls in answering 'wh' questions, it suggests that the programme has had a general effect upon the children's perception and use of language and their knowledge.

The *speech complexity index* is based upon a count of the incidence of certain features in speech the children gave in a semi-structured half-hour interview at age five (see Brandis and Henderson, 1970, for a description of the interview). In a previous experiment we found that there was considerable concordance ($W = 0.75$, $p < 0.001$) in the use of four features likely to be indicative of an 'elaborated code' (Robinson and Creed, 1968; Coulthard and Robinson, 1968): number of subordinate clauses, number of rankshifted clauses, number of verb tenses and number of adverbial groups. The 28 working-class girls were divided on the basis of this complexity. Professor Bernstein had reservations about our use of the term 'elaborated' to refer to the more complex speech of fourteen of the girls, and after two years' consideration we would concur with his preference and label this 'speech complexity'.

The *control and communication index* is described in detail by Bernstein and Brandis (Brandis and Henderson, op. cit.). It differs from the communication index described in Chapter 5 in that it has been supplemented by incorporating information about the mothers' reported strategy for handling discipline problems (see Cook, 1971) and their attitude to toys. In brief, mothers who avoided non-verbal techniques of control and who opted for verbal appeals based upon the affective and overt behavioural consequences for individuals involved in the discipline situations and those who value the explorative use of toys are given high scores. These control scores were incorporated into the communication index, and standardized with a mean of 100 and a standard deviation of 20. This index will be referred to as C.C.I. It was not available when this investigation was planned, but the scores became available for incorporation into the partial correlation matrices. Where children had no C.C.I. score, they were assigned the mean score of the sub-group in which they were included.

Selection of subjects

The original sampling displayed degrees of optimism and pessimism, both of which made simple comparisons difficult when the actual results were obtained.

The major difficulty arose from the unavoidable fact that the children from the middle-class area were a year younger than those in the working-class borough, and so the collection of data from the middle-class area had to be delayed for a year. It could have happened that such data would not be obtained for economic or administrative reasons, and the precaution was taken of having sub-groups of working-class children for internal comparisons in the event of the major social-class contrast being impossible. This meant that we deliberately chose a heterogeneous sample of working-class children, but hoped that the differences between the middle- and the working-class children would swamp the within-working-class variance.

GIRLS

Within the working-class area two independent variables were used: (1) participation in the 'Use of Language' programme, and (2) complexity of speech at age five. Four sub-groups of seven girls each were extracted from the total available sample, so that they were as working-class as possible, but made E.P.V.T. scores with which a middle-class group could subsequently be matched. The

TABLE 7.1 *Sample characteristics: girls*

	Working class			Middle class		
	Social class	E.P.V.T.	C.C.I.	Social class	E.P.V.T.	C.C.I.
Group 1, *language programme, complex speech:*						
	6	94				
	8	102	89			
	9	85	75			
	5	91	84			
	9	91				
	6	96	92			
	8	100	119			
Mean	7·3	94·2	91·8	2	95	103
				2	116	155
Group 2, *language programme, simple speech:*				1	113	151
	8	106	90	2	89	80
	6	97	131	2	101	80
	9	95	101	2	101	110
	9	85	101	1	108	135
	6	104	116	2	119	108
	5	102	118	1	113	131
	8	91	186	3	106	137
Mean	7·3	97·1	120·4	4	91	109
				2	107	109
Group 3, *no language programme, complex speech:*				3	96	118
	7	102	91	3	104	115
	4	95	102	4	115	141
	6	92	109	2	98	115
	4	91	121	2	104	117
	8	103	109	4	104	125
	8	98	94	4	95	103
	6	88	86	3	98	112
Mean	6·1	95·6	101·7	2	119	142
				4	Refusal	114
Group 4, *no language programme, simple speech:*				4	95	105
	8	87	100	5	92	109
	8	103	126	5	104	124
	5	88	109	5	92	130
	8	96	113	5	92	107
	9	91	54	5	106	115
	8	101	123			
	6	86	71			
Mean	7·4	93·1	99·4			
Grand Means	7·0	95·0	104·23	Means 3·0	102·7	117·9

sub-groups were matched as closely as possible on social-class and E.P.V.T. scores.

A year later it was possible to interview the middle-class girls. Twenty-eight were selected to maximize the social-class contrast, but match as far as possible on E.P.V.T. scores.

Table 7.1 shows the sample characteristics. The mean E.P.V.T. score of the middle-class group is higher, but one parameter had to be relaxed and this seemed the least important. C.C.I. scores are also presented, although these were used only in the correlational analysis.

BOYS

The sampling of boys was made very difficult by the rarity of middle-class ones in the working-class borough. Matching on E.P.V.T. added a further constraint, and the final comparison samples contained 11 boys in each of three sub-groups: (1) middle-class, middle-class area; (2) middle-class, working-class area; (3) working-class, working-class area.

Treatment of results

Two main strategies of analysis were employed. The first concentrated upon establishing differences between selected sub-groups of subjects and relied upon such non-parametric and parametric tests as seemed most appropriate, bearing in mind the scale characteristics of the data and a wish to standardize the form in which the results could be presented. The second strategy was to calculate correlation coefficients between the major independent variables and the speech data, with subsequent partialling-out procedures being used to isolate true sources of variance. The strategy was only partly successful, for reasons advanced in Chapter 8.

The results are presented in the following order:

(1) Social-class differences in girls. The experimental design rendered these comparisons the most likely to give reliable and valid results.

(2) The relevance of the 'Use of Language' programme and 'speech complexity' to the performance of working-class girls.

(3) Social-class differences in boys. Initial design errors rendered these comparisons weak, both because of the small numbers of subjects and because of the possible high within-group variance related to intelligence test scores. Class contrasts are made within a working-class area and against middle-class boys living in a middle-class area.

(4) The correlational associations between social class, the control

TABLE 7.2   Sample characteristics: boys

	Middle class, middle-class area			Middle class, working-class area			Working class, working-class area		
	Social class	E.P.V.T.	C.C.I.	Social class	E.P.V.T.	C.C.I.	Social class	E.P.V.T.	C.C.I.
	1	117	141	5	112	120	7	117	113
	2	124	119	5	121	113	8	128	66
	1	101	149	5	102	117	8	105	135
	1	116	119	5	109		9	115	
	2	86	128	5	90		7	93	99
	2	109	154	4	89	105	8	112	80
	2	117	112	3	122	109	7	112	
	2	105	124	5	79	113	8	103	82
	4	105	116	4	114		7	103	146
	2	96	125	5	113		8	82	106
	4	111	127	4	108		7	101	126
Means, 2.1		107·9		4·5	105·4		7·6	106·5	

and communication index and verbal intelligence test scores in (a) girls and (b) boys.

3 Results

Girls

(a) SOCIAL CLASS

In making social-class comparisons for girls, we had the option of contrasting the 28 middle-class girls with the 28 working-class girls or with the 14 working-class girls who had not participated in the 'Use of Language' programme. The first tactic boosts the numbers of subjects, but lessens the chances of finding 'true' differences if the language programme has had a successful influence, while the second tactic reduces the numbers of girls involved. We present both sets of results, but argue mainly from the comparisons with the 14 working-class, since the programme does appear to have had an influence.

The results are presented in Table 7.3, and in our view give a fair representation of the calculations made. For example, for 'why' questions we counted first responses alone as well as first, second and third together. This made little difference, so we confine our presentation to summed responses.

Context

Contextual inappropriateness did not show the predicted difference, but contextual completeness did. Our single index of odd contextual presupposition also differentiated between the groups: working-class girls were more likely to use human-centred appeals to consequences for physical events, e.g. 'The sea has waves so that we can swim in it'.

Mode

For two 'when' questions the predicted middle-class preference for relatively objective modes occurred, but for Q.11, 'When did you start school?' their tendency was to choose answers in mode 3, 'When I was five'. This is an illustration perhaps of a mode bias contingent upon the nature of the question, a point to be taken up later. For 'where' there were no significant differences on individual questions, but also little variance. Over the three questions there was a significant difference, in that the working-class girls were less likely to use names of places (mode 1?). The teaching question showed a middle-class preference for the use of the teacher's name.

TABLE 7.3 *Use of linguistic features by social class, language programme and speech complexity: girls*

| Level of analysis | Linguistic feature, Q. content | % S's using features | | | | Test | M.C.v. W.C. (Con.) | p | M.C.v. W.C. (Total) | p | L.P. | Speech Com-plexity |
		M.C.	W.C. (L.P.)	W.C. (Con)	W.C. (Total)							
Context	Non-why: inappropriateness	42·9	42·9	50·0	46·4	U*	3·1	·01	2·3	·01	=	+
	15: completeness (>2)	67·9	57·1	21·4	39·3						+	−
Mode	1, When: objective	82·1	71·4	35·7	53·6	x^2	13·0	·01	4·3	·05	+	+
	18, When: objective, precise	75·0	35·7	28·6	32·1	x^2	6·5	·02	8·7	·01	++	++
	11, When: mode 3 relative	53·6	42·9	21·4	32·1	x^2	2·7	·1	1·8		++	++
	1, 11, 18, When: modes other than above	14·3	28·6	57·1	42·9	x^2	6·4	·02	4·3	·05		
	2, 4, 6, Where: absence of place names	67·9	78·6	100	89·3	U	2·6	·01	2·0	·05	+	++
	9, Who: teacher's name	57·1	14·3	14·3	14·3	x^2	5·4	·05	9·4	·01	=	
	Physical why, 16, 23, 25, 27 Mode 8: categorization	75·0	57·1	21·4	39·3	U	3·0	·01	2·4	·01	+	−+−
	Mode 9: cause	67·9	42·9	42·9	42·9	U	2·1	·02	1·1		=	=++
	16, mode 8: categorization	67·9	64·3	21·4	42·9	x^2	6·3	·02	2·6		+	
	16, mode 9: cause, correct	57·1	42·9	7·1	25·0	x^2	7·7	·01	4·7	·05	++	
	23, mode 3: regularity alone	17·9	42·9	35·7	39·3	x^2	3·3	·1	2·2		++	
	23, mode 3: regularity plus	17·9	7·1	0	3·6	x^2	·7		1·8		−	
	Social why 21, mode 10: beard prevention	78·6	57·1	28·6	42·9	x^2	7·9	·01	2·5	·01	+	+
	Moral why, 14, 20, 26, 29 Mode 5: authority, specified	10·7	7·1	0	3·6						·+	
	Mode 5: authority, unspecified	14·3	28·6	35·8	32·1						+	+
	Mode 6: wants and wishes	35·7	28·6	14·3	21·4	x^2	1·2				++	+−

	L.P.	Con.			Test	value	p	x²	p	14 v.14 (p<·05)	14 v.14 (p=·005)
Mode 8: categorization (simple)	17·9	35·7	42·9	39·3	x²	1·9	·01	x²,3·87 / 1·9	·05	+	—
Mode 10: consequence											
Avoidance of punishment	21·4	92·9	57·1	75·0	U	3·2	·01			—	+
29, Actor-oriented positive	3·6	21·4	21·4	21·4	x²			2·4	·01	=	—
29, Actor-oriented negative other than punishment	21·4	0	7·1	3·6	Fisher						+
Other-oriented	85·7	57·1	50·0	53·6	U	2·4	·01			+	—
Modes 6 or 10: Other-oriented	89·3	57·1	50·0	53·6	x²	5·9	·02	7·1	·01	+	+
Physical why: irrelevant	42·9	71·4	78·6	75·0	U	3·0	·01	3·4	·01	+	+
Why: don't know (>2)	78·6	50·0	64·3	57·1	U		·02	2·3	·02	—	—
Non-why: inappropriateness (>1)	25·0	57·1	35·7	46·4	U	2·1	·02	1·8	·05	—	—
Who, where, when: incompleteness (nominal group (>1))	17·9	35·7	71·4	53·6				6·3	·01		+
Non-why: incompleteness (>1) (verbal and adverbial groups).	14·3	50·0	42·9	46·4	x²	5·2	·05	5·4	·05	—	=
Non-why: inappropriateness	46·4	71·4	57·1	64·3	x²	5·4	·05	1·2	·02	—	+
Non-why: 'thing' at head	57·1	28·6	14·3	21·4	x²	3·3	·1	6·1		+	=
Non-why: verb, pronoun vagueness	28·6	28·6	0	14·3	x²					=	+
n	28	14	14	28	28					14 v.14	14 v.14

Key: L.P.: Language programme, children
Con.: Control group
Under L.P. and speech complexity, + means difference in direction of middle class, '=' is equal, '—' away. Only 0·1, 0·05, 0·02 and 0·01 probability levels are used

* For U tests values given are for z.

K

'Why' questions gave a number of predicted differences. Appeals to analogy, denials of oddity and appeals to essence virtually did not occur, so no calculations could be made; but for physical questions the middle class were more likely to give causal answers or cite super-ordinate principles of categorization, e.g. 'It's the effect of gravity'. There are weak trends for working-class girls to make appeals to regularity alone, but for middle-class girls to supplement such appeals. For the shaving question, they were more likely to appeal to the hairy consequence of not using a razor. It was the appeals to consequence which gave the significant differences in moral questions also, although sub-category breaks were necessary to reveal this. The working-class girls were particularly concerned about themselves being punished and receiving personal rewards for obeying parents. The middle class, on the other hand, were more concerned about the effects their actions had upon other people.

A number of other modes showed predicted trends which are reported because they achieve significance in the correlational analysis. Where appeals to authority are given, although there is little difference overall, a sub-division based on whether the authority is specified or not (usually a person) shows a greater tendency for the middle class to specify the basis of the authority. Direct appeals to wants and wishes are non-significantly more common in the middle class, while categorization, which for moral questions invariably lacked explanatory force, e.g. 'Because it's naughty', showed a reverse trend. We have already noted the working-class tendency to use the inappropriate (mode 10) human-centred appeal for physical questions, and may add that the working class gave more irrelevant answers to 'why' questions.

Form-grammar

Our index of inappropriateness and the two indices of grammatical incompleteness both gave the significant differences predicted. Presupposition did not.

Form-lexis

Neither inappropriateness nor incompleteness gave the predicted results. Under this heading we repeated the calculation based on our observation of mothers' answers that the middle class were more likely to use 'thing' at head in a nominal group and found the same difference in the girls with a similar tendency for vague verbs and pronouns.

A final observation is that, although there were no class differences in the 'no answer' category, the middle-class girls were more likely to make an explicit statement that they did not know the answer to a question.

(b) *'USE OF LANGUAGE PROGRAMME' AND 'SPEECH COMPLEXITY':*

It would have been possible to run a series of appropriate statistical tests isolating the relevance of these two variables across the individual scores, but we had no computer programme to assist and there were other problems pressing.

What we did was to select those scores which showed social-class differences or a significant association with social class in the correlational analysis, and, taking this list, we asked on how many features the 'language programme' or 'complex speech' children made scores in the predicted direction relative to their comparison group, and how many not. A binomial test could then be applied to assess whether or not this distribution exceeded chance expectation.

We avoided double counting two summary scores (both favourable to a rejection of the null hypothesis), and it emerged that girls who had participated in the 'Use of Language' programme were more like the middle-class girls on 18 features, less like them on 7 and equal on 5. Contrasting the 18 and 7 on a binomial test gives a significant difference ($p = 0.044$).

A similar count on Speech Complexity gives 19 more like the middle class, 8 less like and 3 equal, a nearly significant difference ($p = 0.055$).

Boys

(c) *SOCIAL CLASS*

Although not many of the differences between working- and middle-class boys are significant, Table 7.4 does show results of reasonable similarity to the social differences in girls, strengthening one's persuasion that the class differences are real, and leaving a regret that the design is not strong enough to demonstrate them more adequately.

Context

There are significant differences at the level of context, but while that for completeness is the same as for girls and in line with theoretical expectation, contextual inappropriateness gave a significant difference in the reverse direction.

Mode

Again the differences are similar to those for girls, but fewer in number. Appeals to simple categorization came out in a direction opposite to that expected, but the appeals to attributes of actions and persons gave a class difference not found with girls.

Form

Grammatical and lexical incompleteness gave significant differences in the predicted direction.

Social class differences within a working-class borough

When a binomial test was applied to the scores shown in Table 7.4, on a null hypothesis that if social class is irrelevant there should be no difference in the number of middle-class scores from the working-class area above and below the working-class scores, a significant difference was found overall ($p = 0·012$), and if we drop one of the instances because it involves a double count, the significance of the difference is increased ($p = 0·002$).

(d) CORRELATION MATRICES

Sixty-four scores were selected from the total set of answer scores available for correlational analyses. The objectives of these analyses were several:

(1) By partialling out various possible behavioural correlates of the answer scores, viz. social class, control and communication index, and verbal intelligence test scores, we could examine the residual linguistic relationships in the answering behaviour of seven-year-old children (Chapter 10).

(2) By the time the analyses of differences had been completed, control and communication index scores were available for each child. These could be included in matrices, and by using a partialling technique we were able to assess the relative contribution of social class and the C.C.I. Does the index alone account for most of the variance in the answering behaviour of children or is there much variance still hidden under the social-class blanket?

With boys particularly the relevance of intelligence test scores could be examined; for girls the variance was relatively low.

The results are presented in Tables 7.5 and 7.6.

Girls

Without partialling, 20 linguistic features correlated significantly with social class, 5 with C.C.I. and 8 with intelligence test scores. For social class the results are comparable to the significant differences

TABLE 7.4 *Use of linguistic features by middle- and working-class boys*

Level of analysis	Linguistic feature, Q. Content	Mean incidence of use M.C.	Mean incidence of use W.C.	Fisher test p value	Mean incidence M.C. in W.C. area	Direction of difference
Context	Non-why: inappropriateness	1·00	0·27	<0·05	0·27	=
	15: completeness	5·18	4·18		5·09	+
Mode	2, 4, 6, Where: absence of place-names	0·82	1·55	<0·05	1·46	+
	1, 18, When: objective	1·45	1·00	<0·05	1·17	+
	9, Who, teacher's name	0·55	0·09	<0·05	0·45	+
	Physical why, 16, 23, 25, 27					=
	Mode 9: cause	6·45	5·36		5·36	
	Social why, 23					+
	Mode 10: beard prevention	0·82	0·17	<0·01	0·91	
	Moral why, 14, 20, 26, 29					+
	Mode 6: wants and wishes	1·00	0·17	<0·05	0·27	=
	Mode 8: categorization, action	3·00	2·17	<0·1	3·00	+
	Mode 8: categorization, persons	1·17	0·36	<0·1	0·73	=
	Mode 8: categorization (simple)	2·55	1·82		2·55	
	Mode 10: consequence					+
	Avoidance of punishment to self	2·36	3·09	<0·1	2·27	−
	Other-oriented	2·91	1·64		1·27	−
	Mode 6 or 10: Other-oriented	3·73	1·73	<0·05	1·46	
Non-responses	Physical, why: irrelevant	3·00	3·73	<0·1	3·27	+
Form grammar	Non-why: inappropriateness	1·27	1·64		1·45	+
	Non-why: incompleteness	1·45	2·91	<0·05	1·73	+
Form lexis	Non-why: inappropriateness	0·73	1·00		0·45	+
	Non-why: incompleteness	1·17	1·91	<0·1	1·64	+
	Non-why: 'thing' at head	1·45	1·00		1·17	+
n		11	11		11	

TABLE 7.5 (i) *Linguistic features in relation to social-class, C.C.I. and intelligence-test scores: girls. Correlations and partial correlations (n = 56).*

Question	Content	Mean	S.D.	S.C.	S.C. minus C.C.I. & I.Q	C.C.I.	C.C.I. minus S.C. & I.Q.	I.Q.	I.Q. minus S.C. & C.C.I.
	Social class: high 9, low 0*	5·02	2·50	1·00	1·00	33†	0	47†	0
	English picture vocabulary test	98·64	8·58	47†	0	50†	0	1·00	1·00
	C.C.I.	110·61	22·27	33†	0	1·00	1·00	50†	0
Context									
non-why	Inappropriateness	0·61	0·78	−21	−09	−25	−13	−25	−11
15	Completeness	4·16	2·37	28†	15	45†	36†	26	−01
Mode									
1	When (1), objective, precise or vague	0·68	0·47	29†	18	23	10	26†	10
1	When (2 or 3), relative	0·23	0·43	−15	−08	−15	−07	−16	−06
11	When (3), relative to self	0·43	0·50	15	14	17	17	02	−13
11	When (1 or 2), all other modes	0·39	0·49	−35†	−27†	−26	−15	−21	01
18	When (1), objective, precise	0·59	0·50	54†	46†	30†	14	31†	01
18	When (1, 2, 3), objective vague or relative	0·13	0·33	−30†	−17	−16	04	−34†	−23
2,4,6	Where (1), absence of place -names	1·23	0·83	−32†	−32†	−17	−12	−06	15
2	Where (1), objective	0·95	0·23	13	04	19	12	17	06
4	Where (1), objective or relative to Q.2 answer	0·64	0·48	−01	−08	20	19	09	01
6	Where (1), objective or relative to Q.2 or 4 answer	0·39	0·49	29†	23	06	07	19	09
6	Where, name of sweet-shop	0·18	0·39	00	06	−03	02	−10	−11
2,4,6	Where, use of 'up' and 'down'	0·46	0·74	17	25	−14	−15	−07	−10

Code	Variable	Mean	S.D.						
2,4,6	Where use of 'round'	0·20	0·44	-37†	-34†	-21	-12	-15	08
9	Who, teacher's name	0·36	0·48	53†	44†	22	-02	37†	16
P, M, S	Why (2), restatement of question as answer	2·18	1·78	08	10	12	02	-02	-07
P,M,S	Why (3), regularity	0·54	0·57	-25	-34†	05	05	09	21
23	Why (3), regularity, alone	0·29	0·46	-28†	-30†	-12	-10	-02	-17
23	Why (3), regularity, qualified	0·09	0·29	20	09	17	-04	29†	22
P,M,S	Why (5), authority	0·95	1·37	-06	-03	-09	-07	-06	-00
M	Why (5), authority, specified	0·11	0·37	18	18	-06	-14	07	04
M	Why (5), authority, unspecified	0·43	0·89	-29†	-22	-11	02	-21	-09
M	Why (6), wants and wishes: positive	0·16	0·46	08	22	-20	-15	-19	-19
M	Why (6), wants and wishes: negative	0·25	0·55	10	08	22	25	00	-15
P, M, S	Why (8), categorization, all	4·50	2·14	-05	02	-20	-18	-09	00
P	Why (8), categorization, all	0·95	0·86	16	11	13	08	11	00
M	Why (8), categorization, all	3·52	1·86	-15	-05	-31†	-26	-17	00
	Why (8), categorization, simple	1·73	1·37	-09	05	-19	-07	-27†	-21
	Why (8), categorization of objects	0·39	0·62	04	01	-06	-12	09	13
	Why (8), categorization of actions	2·71	1·70	-03	10	-26	-20	-19	-10
	Why (8), categorization of persons	0·41	0·71	-37†	-37†	-14	-08	07	14
13	Why (9), cause, proximal	0·59	0·68	04	09	-01	04	-09	-13
13	Why (9), cause, distal	1·16	1·26	-05	-05	10	13	-03	-06
P	Why (9), cause, all	3·23	2·18	19	15	-01	-12	15	11
P,M,S	Why (9), cause, all	1·57	1·80	05	05	-00	-00	02	01

Key: S.C. = social class C.C.I. = control and communication index P = physical M = moral
S.D. = standard deviation I.Q. = English picture vocabulary scores S = social † = $p < 0.05$

* Social-class scores have been reversed so that positive correlations mean that high social class is associated with a high score on the variable.

TABLE 7.5 (i) (continued) Linguistic features in relation to social-class, C.C.I. and intelligence-test scores: girls. Correlations and partial correlations (n = 56).

Question	Content	Mean	S.D.	S.C.	S.C. minus C.C.I.&I.Q.	C.C.I.	C.C.I. minus S.C.&I.Q.	I.Q.	I.Q. minus S.C.&C.C.I.
P, M, S	Why (10), consequence, all	4·05	2·17	−14	−15	−11	−11	−01	11
P	Why (10), consequence, all	1·11	1·47	−18	−20	−12	−13	02	17
S	Why (10), consequence, all	1·52	0·87	03	04	−04	−05	−01	−01
M	Why (10), consequence, all	4·11	2·47	−12	−11	−08	−09	01	10
M	Why (10), consequence, positive	0·20	0·44	−10	−01	−02	10	−21	−21
M	Why (10), consequence, negative	1·04	1·11	18	09	19	10	18	06
M	Why (10), consequence, actor-oriented, punishment	1·80	1·69	−47†	−41†	−21	−07	−24	01
M	Why (10), consequence, actor-oriented, other ills	0·52	1·08	01	−05	−10	−19	15	21
M	Why (10), consequence, actor oriented	2·52	2·10	−39†	−34†	−22	−13	−17	06
M	Why (10), consequence, other-oriented	1·41	1·59	31†	25	20	10	17	01
M	Why (10), consequence, action-oriented	0·39	0·65	07	03	−08	−17	14	18
M	Why (6 or 10), appeals to wants of or effects on others	1·79	1·96	28†	26	18	12	09	−09
Non-answers									
Non-why	No answers	0·30	0·93	−04	−05	−02	−01	00	03
P, M, S	No answers	2·23	2·89	−09	−06	05	13	−10	−11

	mean	S.D.						
Non-why — Don't know	0·57	1·11	−20	−12	−08	03	−20	−13
P, M, S — Don't know	4·54	3·19	29†	26	26	21	11	−12
P — Irrelevant answer	1·09	1·40	−50†	−49†	−14	−03	−14	12
Form-grammar								
Non-why Inappropriateness	1·21	0·91	−12	−20	−04	−11	14	25
Non-why Incompleteness	2·59	1·87	−44†	−40†	−21	−11	−17	−08
Non-why Presupposition less than maximal	2·80	1·60	−01	−06	15	14	05	−00
Non-why Mistakes including discord	0·79	1·37	−05	−09	32†	40†	−05	−20
Non-why Substitution	0·13	0·33	−02	03	−14	−12	−07	−01
Form-lexis								
Non-why Inappropriateness	0·95	1·13	−15	−02	−15	−02	−27†	−20
Non-why Incompleteness	1·23	1·26	02	04	13	19	−08	−18
Non-why Presupposition	1·21	1·23	20	20	22	23	01	−19
Non-why Substitution	0·34	0·48	05	10	−08	−07	−07	−07
Non-why Vague lexis: 'thing' 'do' 'get'	0·73	1·00	34†	22	38†	26†	28†	03
10 Functional definition of school	0·84	0·37	21	13	11	−02	22	14

Key: S.C. = social class   C.C.I = control and communication index   P = physical   M = moral
S.D. = standard deviation   I.Q. = English picture vocabulary scores   S = social   † = $p < 0.05$

* Social-class scores have been reversed so that positive correlations mean that high social class is associated with a high score on the variable.

TABLE 7.5 (ii) *Linguistic features in relation to social class, control and communication index, and intelligence-test scores: boys. Correlations and partial correlations (n = 33).*

Question	Content	Mean	S.D.	S.C.	S.C. minus I.C.C.I. & Q.	C.C.I.	C.C.I. minus S.C. & I.Q.	I.Q.	I.Q. minus S.C. & C.C.I.
	Social class: high 9, low 0*	4·76	2·44	1·00	1·00	54†	0	07	0
	English picture vocabulary test	106·58	12·11	07	0	−14	0	1·00	1·00
	C.C.I.	115·79	18·34	54†	0	1·00	1·00	−14	0
Context									
Non-why	Inappropriateness	0·52	0·71	38†	36†	19	−06	−14	−19
15	Completeness	4·82	2·27	12	19	01	−13	−25	−29
Mode									
1	When (1), objective, precise or vague	0·79	0·42	27	34	−01	21	−07	−13
1	When (2 or 3), relative	0·18	0·39	−38†	−47†	−05	27	21	31
11	When (3), relative to self	0·52	0·51	02	05	−05	−06	05	04
11	When (1 or 2), all other modes	0·42	0·50	−06	−08	05	07	−16	−14
18	When (1), objective, precise	0·52	0·51	27	28	10	−08	−07	−11
18	When (1, 2, 3), objective, vague relative	0·12	0·33	−08	−10	02	07	−03	−01
2, 4, 6	Where (1), absence of place-names	1·27	0·94	−40†	−27	−29	−14	−16	−18
2	Where (1), objective	0·88	0·33	15	11	10	02	03	03
4	Where (1), objective or relative to Q.2 answer	0·70	0·47	−02	07	−14	−15	02	−01
6	Where (1), objective or relative to Q.2 or answer	0·21	0·42	29	22	18	04	04	03
6	Where, name of sweet-shop	0·33	0·48	−29	−34	−00	20	−00	06
2, 4, 6	Where, use of 'up' and 'down'	0·39	0·70	05	08	04	−04	−20	−21

		Mean	S.D.						
2, 4, 6	Where, use of 'round'	0·21	0·48	−07	−06	−05	−00	04	05
9	Who, teachers name	0·36	0·49	32	29	23	01	−26	−29
P, M, S	Why (2), restatement of question as answer	3·30	2·32	−20	−06	−24	−19	−10	−12
P, M, S	Why (3), regularity	0·61	0·61	−12	−06	−17	−10	12	11
23	Why (3), regularity, alone	0·15	0·36	−01	08	−03	−11	−36†	−38†
23	Why (3), regularity, qualified	0·24	0·44	15	−02	23	24	29	33
P, M, S	Why (5), authority	1·30	1·53	−06	−04	−08	−03	12	12
M	Why (5), authority, specified	0·06	0·24	19	20	04	−08	−00	−03
M	Why (5), authority, unspecified	0·61	1·09	−14	01	−28	−23	12	08
M	Why (6), wants and wishes: positive	0·27	0·57	38†	19	44†	28	−07	−04
M	Why (6), wants and wishes: negative	0·21	0·48	33	20	33	17	−12	−11
P, M, S	Why (8), categorization, all	5·52	2·75	18	14	08	02	17	16
P	Why (8), categorization, all	2·09	1·26	04	01	01	03	19	18
M	Why (8), categorization, all	3·61	2·36	20	18	06	−04	10	08
	Why (8), categorization, simple	2·30	1·78	15	14	05	−03	07	05
	Why (8), categorization of objects	0·24	0·56	−11	−08	−10	−04	03	03
	Why (8), categorization of actions	2·70	1·96	13	14	−01	−07	15	13
	Why (8), categorization of persons	0·94	1·34	12	−01	24	20	−10	−06

Key: S.C. = social class   C.C.I = control and communication index   P = physical   M = moral
      S.D. = standard deviation   I.Q. = English picture vocabulary scores   S = social   † = $p < 0.35$

* Social-class scores have been reversed so that positive correlations mean that high social class is associated with a high score on the variable.

TABLE 7.5 (ii) (continued) Linguistic features in relation to social class, control and communication index, and intelligence test scores: boys. Correlations and partial correlations (n = 33)

Question	Content	Mean	S.D.	S.C.	S.C. minus C.C.I. & I.Q.	C.C.I.	C.C.I. minus S.C. & I.Q.	I.Q.	I.Q. minus S.C. & C.C.I.
13	Why (9), cause, proximal	1·12	1·14	−15	−20	06	15	−09	−05
13	Why (9), cause distal	1·42	1·15	17	21	−04	−14	19	16
P	Why (9), cause, all	5·73	2·39	19	01	25	25	27	31
P, M, S	Why (9), cause, all	4·52	2·77	14	03	15	15	24	26
P, M, S	Why (10), consequence, all	4·73	2·43	10	−12	32	34	09	17
P	Why (10), consequence, all	0·48	1·06	−06	−06	01	04	−08	−07
S	Why (10), consequence, all	1·48	0·91	16	23	−11	−20	19	14
M	Why (10), consequence, all	5·18	2·57	15	−07	33	32	10	17
M	Why (10), consequence, positive	0·30	0·68	−05	−19	15	−25	13	19
M	Why (10), consequence, negative	1·36	1·58	14	−04	26	27	17	22
M	Why (10), consequence, actor-oriented, punishment	2·58	1·98	−18	−15	−07	01	−11	−10
M	Why (10), consequence, actor-oriented, other ills	0·48	0·80	07	−03	15	15	05	08
M	Why (10), consequence, actor oriented	3·15	1·73	−16	−17	−02	07	−07	−04
M	Why (10), consequence, other-oriented	1·94	2·12	28	−05	51†	49†	19	30
M	Why (10), consequence, action-oriented	0·67	1·41	15	−00	27	23	03	07
M	Why (6 or 10), appeals to wants of or effects on others	2·33	2·50	37†	06	55†	49†	15	26

		Mean	S.D.						
Non-answers									
Non-why	No answers	0·03	0·17	06	08	−03	−07	02	00
P, M, S	No answers	0·70	1·42	−07	−02	−04	−05	−24	−24
Non-why	'Don't know'	0·48	0·83	26	26	18	−02	−28	−31
P, M, S	'Don't know'	2·27	2·67	13	33	−25	−38†	−07	−02
P	Irrelevant answers	0·88	1·43	−09	−06	01	00	−35†	−34
Form-grammar									
Non-why	Inappropriateness	1·48	0·76	−22	−23	00	10	−26	−23
Non-why	Incompleteness	2·03	1·45	−45†	−46†	−10	17	−19	−15
Non-why	Presupposition less than maximal	2·52	1·33	−09	−20	14	23	−02	04
Non-why	Mistakes including discord	1·21	1·60	11	17	12	−06	−34	−55†
Non-why	Substitution	0·18	0·39	05	−05	13	15	12	14
Form-lexis									
Non-why	Inappropriateness	0·73	0·94	−17	−11	−15	−06	−00	−00
Non-why	Incompleteness	1·58	1·66	−20	−17	−14	−01	16	17
Non-why	Presupposition	1·24	1·30	03	−07	17	18	−03	01
Non-why	Substitution	0·24	0·44	−26	−44†	18	40†	−08	02
Non-why	Vague lexis: 'thing', 'do', 'get'	1·21	1·71	01	01	05	02	−14	−13
10	Functional definition of school	0·79	0·42	11	24	−12	−25	−12	−18

Key: S.C. = social class   C.C.I = control and communication index   P = physical   M = moral
      S.D. = standard deviation   I.Q. = English picture vocabulary scores   S = social   † = $p < 0.05$

* Social-class scores have been reversed so that positive correlations mean that high social class is associated with a high score on the variable.

found with x^2 and U tests, both in number and type. Some extra relationships were found: an objective mode for 'where' answers being more common in the middle class; the use of regularity alone, appeals to unspecified authority, categorizations of persons and the use of 'round' in 'round the corner' being associated with the working class.

Intelligence test scores and C.C.I. have a disappointingly low number of correlates with linguistic features. Partialling out the other two independent variables leaves C.C.I. with three significant correlates and intelligence test scores with none. Social class is left with 12 and generally it appears that partialling has less effect on social class than on the other variables.

The conclusion would appear to be that, although C.C.I. has relationships to answering behaviour, social class has stronger associations, and the particular features of social class relevant to variations in answering remain under the blanket.

Boys

Similar but much weaker results were found with the boys. Social class had 6 significant correlations (4 partials), C.C.I. 3 (but virtually 2) (4 partials), and intelligence test scores 2 (2 partials). The partial correlations added little to our knowledge, except that lexical substitution was found to be less common in the middle class.

4 Discussion

We commented in the Introduction (see p. 119) with sufficient adverse criticism against the design of the investigation to render further comment masochistic. We suspect that in behavioural studies with many dependent variables and multiple determinants, the design problems are only overcome by using very large samples, quite beyond the usual financial resources of social science research teams. Very tightly controlled experimental studies can cope with problems of specifying the relationships of small numbers of independent and dependent variables when the forms of their relationships are simple, e.g. additive, interactional. Our intermediate strategy opens us to attacks from two directions: not enough subjects and data to produce an impregnable set of differences; not enough control to allow causal inferences. Nevertheless, it will be argued that there are enough predicted differences to support Bernstein's theory and to attest to the empirical validity of much of the taxonomic scheme for answers to 'wh' questions.

The major prediction not confirmed was that which proposed that middle-class children with an elaborated code use of language should have their knowledge and beliefs organized systematically, both with respect to an hierarchical set of higher- and lower-order categories rich in information regarding similarities and differences on a variety of attributes, and with respect to the temporal dimension, emphasizing past and future as well as present states set within a causal framework. It was not that the prediction was disconfirmed, but that the probing of answers to 'why' questions did not give data that could be analysed along these lines. To answer such questions requires a more systematic and sustained cross-examination of suitable children, probably posing questions specifically formulated to elicit a variety of modes, and the associated categories and causal features.

The dependent variables derived from the scheme described in Chapters 2 and 3 stood up well under test, especially in the social-class comparisons.

For context, completeness and a weak index of presupposition showed up class differences. Inappropriateness did, in reverse, but it must be remembered that the answers to the 'non-why' questions were deliberately intended to be within the children's conceptual competence to answer. For the 'why' questions we chose to classify odd answers as 'irrelevant', but in one sense they are more than inappropriate (see p. 23), lacking even the lexical continuity which would enable them to be classified as answers, and if we had elected to call some modes 'inappropriate' as answers to certain questions the category would have differentiated between the classes.

For modes, too, results were generally consistent with expectation, both with 'when' and 'where' and with 'why' questions. Unfortunately class differences in appeals to essence, denials of oddity and appeals to analogy could not be tested, because only very few children used any of these. It could be argued that the situational features did not encourage the use of the last two. For a seven-year-old to deny the reasonableness of an adult interviewer's question would show a rare quality of independent thinking, while appeals to analogy are more likely to occur in a teaching than a 'testing' situation.

The detective work within modes revealed that the original taxonomy was too crude for exposing the full extent of the differences between the groups. This was illustrated in several modes: the middle-class children made appeals to regularity, but were more likely to qualify them; they made appeals to authority, but were more likely to specify its nature; their appeals to consequences in answer to moral questions were more likely to be other than self-oriented, and when they were self-oriented were less concerned with punishment. The extent to which sub-categories of modes are needed, and which ones in particular, will be a function of the subjects used, the type of question asked and the purposes of the investigator, but for our type of problem with young children in our culture, Piaget's pioneering work, with its refinement and extensions exemplified in the work of Lovell (1968) and Kohlberg (1964), to name but two important contributors, offers some sound clues as to the sub-divisions likely to be useful.

Hence our initial predictions about use of modes needs to be supplemented by reference to likely orientations and elaborations within modes.

Our predictions about modes were also made with insufficient attention to the content and context of the question asked. Combinations of factors within the scales of register will operate to make some modes of answer more apposite than others. For example, on some occasions with some participants an answer to a 'when' question in an objective mode would be strange to say the least, e.g. 'When do people get the old age pension in England?' is likely to evoke a reply giving an age reference. Our questions were confined to unique events, but even with one of these, 'When did you start school?' the mode 3 reply 'When I was 5', was the most common— more so in the middle than in the working class. To generate more precise predictions from Bernstein's theory would require a more sophisticated analysis of types and occasions of 'when'—and other questions than we have attempted.

'Why'questions revealed similar complications. Our rough division into physical-natural and moral questions showed this. The physical-natural questions predisposed children to answer in terms of causes and categories, and occasionally consequences, while moral questions gave no first responses which could be described as causal, which is not surprising. Causal answers are more appropriate for empirical than normative matters. It is possible to imagine causal answers, e.g. 'Why should you do what your parents tell you to?' might evoke a reply, 'Because they are always good to me'. However, this might be better construed as an answer to 'Why do you . . . ?' rather than 'Why should you . . . ?' Again, the implication is that to utilize the taxonomic scheme for making specific predictions from Bernstein's, or another, sociolinguistic theory will necessitate prior consideration of the relevance of scales of register and their integration into the classification of responses.

Appropriateness and completeness both received empirical support for their utility, while presupposition failed at the formal levels of grammar and lexis. That the middle class were more flexible in their use of language is not indicated by any correlations between class and grammatical or lexical substitution, but it would seem that possible differential capacity or preference for formal presupposition needs to be tested in situations other than the one we used.

A more general evaluation of the taxonomy is presented in Volume II.

From this study it would appear to constitute a sound framework for the analysis of answers to questions, but requiring elaboration and refinement as the occasion demands.

The independent variables differed in the extent of their relationships to the predicted differences in answer to 'wh' questions. Although the 'speech complexity' index taken at age five did not quite achieve significance at the 5 per cent level overall, it was a narrow defeat. The index was based on only four scores obtained from a semi-structured interview two years prior to this investigation and answers to 'wh' questions constitute a very different speech sample. It does not therefore seem unreasonable to conclude that a differential has been maintained over the two years and that the earlier scores have a measure of predictive validity.

With boys social class was shown to be a differentiating variable in answers to 'wh' questions, in spite of the low numbers of subjects and the fact that one group was mainly lower-middle-class. These boys were in the same schools as the working-class group and much of their extra-familial environment may be assumed to be similar, implying, but not proving, the importance of the intra-familial environment as a source of determinants of speech characteristics.

That the 'Use of Language' programme girls were significantly more like the middle-class comparison group than the control group children was particularly gratifying, especially since the programme had had no special emphasis upon answering 'wh' questions. It does suggest that a cheap, easy-to-run intervention procedure focusing upon use of language can have a generalized effect in a comparatively short time.

The correlation matrices gave only weak associations between aspects of answers and intelligence test scores. This is hardly surprising for girls where an attempt had been made to reduce the variance in test scores. The same was not true of the boys, but even here few associations were found.

Social class remained the strong variable, even when the C.C.I. and intelligence test scores had been partialled out. The C.C.I. did not produce an impressive array of relationships, and such as there were dropped when the other two variables were partialled out.

L

This result is surprising in two respects. Firstly, other work with the same sample has found this index to have significant associations over and above social class with a variety of behavioural indices (Bernstein and Young, 1967; Brandis and Henderson, 1970), and, secondly, the content of the index, based as it is in part on how the mother reports she handles her children's questions and whether or not she uses verbal appeals in controlling her child's behaviour, would lead us to expect that it was tapping aspects of maternal behaviour directly relevant to the child's likely capacity to answer 'wh' questions. We are not able to claim this, however, and instead are forced to conclude that, although the complex variable of 'social class' does account for variation in children's answers to 'wh' questions, the C.C.I. is not tapping the critical features. This point is taken up again in Chapter 8.

The theoretical basis for the investigation does emerge validated in the main. We were unable to test a number of predictions, especially those concerned with the structure of children's belief systems. The hypotheses concerning formal presupposition and the use of restatements of questions as answers received no support at all. Some others did not achieve significance, but trends were in the right direction in more than one comparison. Contextual inappropriateness gave a difference in an unexpected direction with boys for 'non-why' questions, but the feature was not tested strongly. Otherwise we may summarize the results by saying that the other hypotheses were supported in at least one comparison, and usually more.

Relative to the working-class children, the middle-class children did use:

1 At the level of context, more contextual completeness and less unjustified presupposition.

2 At the level of mode selection:

(a) More objective modes of answering 'when' and 'where' questions (with the reservations mentioned on p. 148 and elaborated in Chapter 9).

(b) More appeals to cause in answer to physical questions, consequence on the shaving question, more other-oriented consequences in answer to the moral questions (but fewer self-oriented punishment avoidance appeals), more appeals to categorization when these were more than 'simple' and fewer when they were not (with one exception). (Although there were no differences overall in appeals to regularity and authority, qualified regularity and specified authority were more common in the middle class and simple regularity and unspecified authority in the working class.) There were fewer irrelevant answers.

3 At the formal level of grammar, less grammatical inappropriateness and incompleteness.

4 At the formal level of lexis, somewhat less lexical inappropriateness and incompleteness.

Chapter 8   Answers to 'wh' questions in relation to Bernstein's theory

We have mentioned some sins of omission and commission in the discussion sections of the previous three chapters, and we postpone our evaluation of the taxonomic scheme from a linguistic point of view for the second volume. Here we try to set out the links between the three empirical investigations reported, and then place the results and inferences in the wider context of the Bernstein theory, making particular reference to relevant work done at the Sociological Research Unit.

Chapters 5 and 7, which reported the studies of children's speech, are complementary and fortunately consistent. Although the study reported in Chapter 5 did no more than scratch at the possible usefulness of the taxonomic scheme, particularly its formal features, it did show significant social-class differences in answering behaviour, with the working-class answers being more concrete, less comprehensive and less cognizant of knowledge and perspectives other than their own. In their explanations of how to play 'Hide-and-seek' the working-class five-year-olds made more unjustified contextual presuppositions. This greater contextual presupposition was also displayed in their undifferentiated use of pronouns to refer to the participants in the game; the interviewer could only infer that 'you' was not used to refer to the same person or persons throughout, because she already knew how to play the game. There are similarities here to Hawkin's (1969) results, which show a higher incidence of pronouns and adjuncts ('here', 'there', etc.), with no precise referents in working-class narrative stories, although in the particular story-telling situation used there were possibilities for the child to communicate by non-verbal means, and hence we would classify such items as signs of lexical incompleteness. These data on contextual presupposition and lexical incompleteness in five-year-olds complement the relative paucity of such data from the older children, where the emphasis fell on the mode and form of answers.

Given the wide range of social-class differences found in answering 'wh' questions across context, mode, grammar and lexis, how do these come to exist? The simplest hypothesis is that the differences reflect differences in what is made available for the children to learn and how it is made available. For young children, both aspects are usually mainly a function of the mothers' behaviour and the environment the family provides.

In this case the form, content and manner of the mothers' handling of the children's questions and their other information-offering activities and opportunities should be most relevant.

We have presented data on how mothers report they would answer their children's questions, and a strong case can be argued that the social-class differences found are likely to be particularly relevant to the differences in the children, on the basis of the similarities between mothers and children.

The middle-class mothers evaded fewer questions, gave more accurate answers with more information in them, more simply presented. The middle-class children offered fewer answers irrelevant to the 'why' questions posed and gave more information, but less accurate information in answer to the 'non-why' questions. The reflection is imperfect. We may also note that the children did not differ in their combined 'No answer—Don't know' responses, but it will be recalled that we deliberately avoided asking questions which we judged would be beyond the children's capacity to answer.

For modes of answer, working-class mothers were more likely to repeat the question as a statement and appeal to simple regularity or authority. Similarly, working-class children were more likely to appeal to simple regularity and unspecified authority, but they were not more likely to restate the question as a statement. This may be a contextual matter, a function of the participants involved; a mother answering her child in this way is providing no information relevant to the content of the question, but may be asserting her authority, whereas a young child answering an interviewer is hardly likely to assume a right to exercise such authority, and the restatement may well serve mainly as a sign only that nothing better can be produced. The middle-class mothers were more likely to appeal to analogy, categorization, cause and consequence (nearly significant alone for boys), and, with appropriate refinements of scoring procedure, the middle-class children behaved similarly. More causal explanations and appeals to more than 'simple' categorization came from them, and we have already noted that appeals to analogy may be used more fittingly in teaching than 'testing' situations. Appeals to consequence were more common in middle-class children for the question asked of both mothers and children about shaving, but for

moral questions more complicated scoring refinements were necessary.

It is probably more appropriate to link the children's answers in
this area to the work of Cook (1971), than to our own study of
mothers' answers (see Chapter 6). She was not dealing with children's
questions, but with control problems, and found that middle-class
mothers were more likely than working-class mothers to make verbal
appeals based upon behavioural and affective consequences for participants, while the working class were more likely to resort to non-verbal
strategies and brief commands (imperatives). Hess and Shipman
(1967) have found similar results in America. These results fit neatly
with the children's answers: the working-class children's preference
for appeals to consequence for the actor, especially those involving
avoidance of punishment—and sensibly so if the mothers' answers
are valid; the middle-class preference for appeals to consequence for
others, or effects upon self other than punishment, again corres-
ponding to what the mothers have claimed to have done. A final
point worth mentioning is that Cook (and others; see Kohlberg,
1964) found that middle-class mothers were more likely to base their
moral judgments upon the intentions of the actor rather than the
consequences of the action, and our middle-class children were more
likely to appeal to states of people, viz. their wants and wishes.

In our opinion, the data from the mothers and children mesh
neatly. The data may be correlational only, but it would be absurdly
sceptical not to infer some causal relationship between the maternal
behaviour and the form and content of the children's answers to
'wh' questions, especially in the absence of a better story. However,
it is appropriate to consider other possible relevant factors.

What then might these determinants be? Clearly, the answer is that
there are many, and even though the sociological rag-bag index of
social class is significantly associated with many features, it is cover-
ing only a small proportion of the variance. Our single attempt to
proceed to the social-psychological level of analysis with the Control
and Communication Index failed, but this perhaps is not surprising.
The index comprised four features of reported mother-child interaction and one attitudinal feature: whether she answered difficult
questions, in how wide a range of situations she was willing to talk
with her child and to what extent she used personal appeals in her
control strategies, to what extent she avoided coercive or imperative
means of control and her attitude to toys. This index may give a
general indication of how much talking goes on, but it leaves out
many aspects of behaviour which are more likely to bear a direct
relationship to the child's behaviour. The prime candidate for inclusion would be an index based on the frequency and quality of the

answers the mother gives in reply to the child's questions. (We did not devise such an index because our priorities were to develop a linguistically based taxonomic scheme for analysing answers to 'wh' questions and test certain aspects of Bernstein's theory against this scheme. It is regrettable that we had neither the time nor a sufficiency of mother-child pairs on whom transcribed data was available to make a thorough test of this possibility. At a later point in time we may be able to undertake such an analysis on a small group of subjects.) But other features are also likely to be relevant. How many questions of what sort does the child ask and are they information-seeking in intent? Is the physical and social environment made rich in objects and events about which questions can be asked, and is the child encouraged to ask them? More generally, does the child come to learn about the referential usage of language and is he taught this efficiently?

The list could be extended, reliable and valid measuring techniques would be required for each, a theoretical model of their likely interactions constructed, and some form of appropriate analysis (e.g. multiple regression) used to maximize predictive validity. Unfortunately, such sophistication was outside our frame of reference.

Meanwhile, it remains for us to locate our work within Bernstein's theoretical framework. One difficulty experienced by many people who have tried to understand his writings stems from their failure to separate out discrete levels of analysis within the social sciences, and a brief résumé along these lines may help locate our studies within the general picture.

There are *sociological* questions about the conditions under which certain groupings of people are likely to generate a restricted code use of language, the form this is likely to take, and why. There are *social psychological* questions about the means by which the code is transmitted from one individual to another, which themselves divide into two levels of analysis: what are the *values and attitudes* governing the behaviour of the transmitting agents and what is the *actual verbal and non-verbal behaviour* they enact which directly influences the recipient. Given that the recipient acquires the restricted code use of language only, we may ask *psychological* questions about the consequences for his perception, thinking, memory, learning and actions in the material world and *social psychological* questions about the same processes in relation to the social world and find out why he should remain confined to the code.

Where the recipient is a child being socialized into a society, we can ask these questions about each of the socializing agents which he encounters: mother, father, siblings, peers, teachers, etc., and we can ask why those significant others who have an elaborated code of language use might succeed or fail in switching the child on to this possibility. For each individual the questions can be posed at a hierarchy of levels from psychological through to sociological, e.g. a child in the educational system might retain only a restricted code of language use because the teachers' behaviour does not promote a switch, perhaps because teachers fail to understand the problem and/or have beliefs about the nature of such children at variance with reality. We can ask how they came to acquire such beliefs and why they maintain them, but as we raise the level of analysis we might arrive at sociologically based functional explanations of the phenomena, e.g. the occupational structure of the society requires different proportions of unskilled, semi-skilled, skilled, etc., labour, and the educational system serves to select and recruit individuals for these jobs—neither under- nor over-educating. All participants in the educational process—parents, peers, pupils, teachers, head-teachers, local educational authorities, and the Department of Education and Science—behave appropriately.

The point of this digression is to argue that the total picture is an hierarchical one, and it is essential to describe each set of features at its appropriate level of analysis and explain them with reference to the level of analysis immediately above and not at several stages away, e.g. social class does not cause children to speak in restricted code.

It is tempting to describe the total picture in detail, but this is beyond our frame of reference, and we must content ourselves with locating our work within it.

Bernstein (1970) has recently made more precise statements about the sociological conditions under which restricted codes are likely to develop, and specified the type of family structure and processes of socialization likely to result in a child's learning only a restricted code use of language. The results obtained are remarkably consistent with his theory.

At the level of *values and attitudes*, data from within the Sociological Research Unit (Bernstein and Young, 1967; Bernstein and Henderson, 1970; Jones, 1966), and outside (see references cited in Chapter 1 p. 11) show that the lower working-class orientation towards education and child-rearing overall, and to language in particular, are consistent with the *sociological* expectations. The *self-reported behaviour* of mothers (Bernstein and Brandis, 1970; Cook, 1971) and the *observed behaviour* of mothers interacting with their children (Hess and Shipman, 1967) confirm the values and attitudes expressed. Our contribution in Chapter 6 is to add to this pool of information by showing how Bernstein's thesis is supported in several predicted ways: working-class mothers reporting how they would answer their children's questions produce responses with a higher incidence of 'no answers', inaccurate and lesser amounts of information in a 'noisy' linguistic context, restatements of questions as answers and appeals to simple regularity and authority. We infer that these mothers are using a restricted code whose function is to specify the form of the mother-child relationship rather than to teach the child about other matters—as Bernstein's theory demands.

The consequences for the working-class children should be that they also use a restricted code in answering 'wh' questions. Our taxonomy of aspects of answering behaviour (Chapters 2 and 3) was used to generate predictions from Bernstein's statements about the functions and forms of the restricted code (Chapter 4), subsequently put to empirical tests (Chapters 5 and 7). The results were persuasively consistent with the hypotheses in most respects: the working-class children showing more contextual incompleteness and unjustified presupposition, an absence of objective modes of answers for certain types of 'where' and 'when' questions, a preference for appeals to simple regularity, unspecified authority, simple categorization, and actor-oriented appeals to consequence (for moral questions), more grammatical inappropriateness and incompleteness and more lexical incompleteness. These are *observed features* of the children's verbal behaviour, whose eventual consequences are not for us to assess here and now, but are consistent with an expectation that these children will not learn as well as they might in school, unless given a rather different education from that which we expect they will receive.

The facts augur well for the continuing success of Bernstein's theory at a variety of levels of analysis. They pose some daunting practical problems for an educational system allegedly intended to provide equal opportunity to all children.

Appendix A   Sample transcripts of mothers' and children's answers

We include four transcripts of one middle-class mother and one working-class mother answering six questions about how she would reply to certain questions posed by her child (see Chapter 6), along with the replies given by their respective children in response to the thirty questions we posed to them when they were seven (see Chapter 7).

Traditional punctuation cannot express the intonational and temporal structure of the replies given, and hence our transcripts fail to convey all the information available on the tape-recordings. Where words or phrases could not be determined we insert . . . , but where a reasonable guess could be hazarded we insert [?] after the guessed word.

As we mentioned in Chapter 1, these samples are not typical in any statistical sense, but neither do they represent extremes. The reader is left to decide which mother and child belong to which social group!

'Q.' stands for question, 'P.' stands for probe, and 'Ans.' stands for answer.

Mrs Smith	*Mrs Cooper* $\cap$. $\subset$.
Q.1 For instance, children sometimes ask why people have to do things. Imagine Sandra asking, 'Why does Daddy shave every morning?' What would you say?	Q.1. Well, children often ask questions. I wonder what you'd say if Giles asked you, 'Why does Daddy shave every morning?'
Ans. Oh I'd try and explain to her, just have to explain to her what is it she calls it? Oh no, that's right, she does	Ans. Oh, I'd say because little hairs grow through his skin because he's a man and that happens to you

Mrs Smith	Mrs Cooper

call them whiskers. She says he's got whiskers under his arms, hasn't he? Don't you? [Conversation with child] and it's been hot weather and he's out in the garden and she [child crying] and she turns round and says to him, 'Daddy, you've got to shave those whiskers off your chest!'

when you're grown up and become a man and it doesn't look very nice so he has to take them off.

Q.2. Supposing Sandra asked, 'Where does the water in the tap come from?' What would you say?

Ans. Ah, try to explain something that, just explain that you'd have to try and explain that it comes through the pipes and through the reservoir. Oh, I can't say that word. I mean children if you try to explain it simple they know all the details, don't they? I mean if you give them a simple explanation, I mean they understand more [?].

Q.2. Imagine him asking, 'Where does the water in the tap come from?'

Ans. Oh, hasn't long pipes under the road which lead into bigger pipes which go right down to the water house [?] in . . . [name] and they pump it up from the river and clean it and it comes all that way [laughs].

Q.3. Here's another one. Imagine Sandra asking, 'Why do leaves fall off the trees?'

Q.3. Imagine him asking, 'Why do leaves fall off the trees?' What would you say?

Ans. I think I'd explain to her that summer's gone, they die at this time of year. She does know why they fall off, she does because she knows that flowers die. You pick them off as they die like now out in the garden and er the same with the tree 'cos it has started to

Ans. Because it's now autumn time and the trees are going to have a rest and these leaves have died and they've come—come away ready for new ones to go in this place.

Mrs Smith   *Mrs Cooper*

---

shed its leaves already and she said, 'Oh it'll soon be winter time'. She associates the leaves coming off the trees, she must do, it's winter.

Q.4.   Children sometimes ask why people act as they do. Imagine Sandra asking, 'Why did Mrs Jones cry when Johnny went to hospital?' What would you say? assuming Mrs Jones was imaginary.

Ans.   I'd think you'd have to explain to her that er oh, I suppose like what we did with us. I explained when my own little girl went into hospital that she cried and all . . . why are you crying because she loves him and worry over him. She cried because she missed her own sister, so I mean with an experience like that it's easier to explain, I think. Of course, if she don't know why then I would, but I mean you've got to explain to them that it's because you miss them. That you cry because they're ill. You'd have to explain it somehow, wouldn't you?

Q.5.   I'm sure you've had this one. Imagine Sandra asking, 'Where do I come from?' What would you say?

Ans.   Well she thinks she comes from under a, no I haven't told her that. Her sister told

Q.4.   Imagine him asking, 'Why did Mrs Jones cry when Johnny went to hospital?'

Ans.   Well, she was very upset and worried about her little boy but he's going to be all right. The nurses and doctors will look after him, but it's a sad thing for a mummy that her little boy's not very well— when he has to go to hospital [laughs].

Q.5.   Imagine Giles asking, 'Where do I come from?'

Ans.   Oh I told him—we've had all this—that he started as a tiny little seed and he's

Mrs Smith	Mrs Cooper

her that she comes from a rose bush but she knows she comes from a hospital. She she automatically thinks that's where she comes from. Yes, 'cos she was saying the other day, 'Are the ladies going in there to collect their babies, Mummy?' See, she thinks you just go in and collect them. She's never bothered to actually ask. No, but I've got that to come yet. I've got that to come.

been shown a packet of seeds and planted them— which grows inside Mummy's tummy and grows and grows. We've had books from the library which illustrate the beauty . . . yes and and . . . em then the baby has grown so much he has everything, you know, eyes, ears and . . . little heart and he's ready to come into the world and start living and being a little person on his own and then we have a long, long [laughs]—'How does it get there?' or 'How does it come out of your tummy?'—er [laughs].

P.   What do you think you'll say when it comes?

Ans. Well I don't know till they ask me I don't know what I'd say. I think you're just as embarrassed as what they are. You have to explain then to tell them the truth or what. But I think most of them the oldest girls know where she's told them. If they don't learn I mean they learn it at school. I mean it stands to reason as they get older, they're not silly.

Q.6. Imagine Sandra asking, 'Who is the man who brings the milk?' What would you say?

Q.6. Er, imagine Giles asking 'Who is the man who brings the milk?'

Mrs Smith	Mrs Cooper
Ans. I suppose you'd tell her it's the milkman. I think she knows. At her age they automatically know. I mean at baby's age she might say who is the man who brings the milk but I couldn't imagine Sandra. She goes out looking for the milkman if he's late. She knows he brings the milk.	Ans. Oh [laughs], well first I'd say he was the milkman and that he was doing his job um he knows that we get milk from cows the farm . . . looks after cows and they give us milk and it goes into big churns— he's seen that and then he's . . . to go to a dairy and then when it's been cleaned and . . . it's put into bottles, he has seen that so he would—so someone very kindly brings it round to us all and he's the milkman.
Q.7. And, finally, imagine Sandra asking, 'Why do I have to go to school in September?' What would you say?	Q.7. Imagine Giles asking, 'Why do I have to go to school in September?'
Ans. Well I don't know I should say, I should say because um she's well um she's five and because she's got to learn. You know her sums and her. She's got to learn her ABC's so that she can grow up. You can't be silly when you grow up, can they? Can they?	Ans. Which he does every day [laughs] and I certainly have said you know you'll find it very happy there Giles there'll be lots of things for you to do and you'll you're going to learn to read and you'll enjoy that you know how Ian and Jane do and then you can belong to the library and you'll be able to write you'll learn to write and you're getting to be a big boy that you really could be able to manage to do these things—and also it's so interesting, lots of girls and boys to play with—

Mrs Smith	*Mrs Cooper*
	we say—I say numerous things to him on those lines and we've seen the lovely pictures—yes— Hallo . . . [child comes in— speech indistinct]

		Giles Cooper	*Sandra Smith*
Q.1.	When do you go home from school?	Four o'clock.	At dinner-time.
Q.2.	Where is your home?	In Chalklands.	Howards Road.
Q.3.	What is a home for?	Er, for you to live in.	Children.
Q.4.	Where does your best friend live?	I don't know.	At th' thirty-four.
P.	You don't know where your best friend lives?	No.	
Q.5.	What is a friend?	A person who you love and like and play with.	A girl.
Q.6.	Where is your favourite sweetshop?	Um. Park Lamby.	Up the top.
Q.7.	How do you buy sweets?	With money.	With money.
Q.8.	How well can you read?	Well, I can read O.K., all right.	Good.
Q.9.	Who gives you lessons at school?	Our teacher.	The teacher.
Q.10.	What is a school?	A place you go to to learn.	A school is for lessons.
Q.11.	When did you start at Infant School?	Um, Northampton.	Last year.
P.	You started in Northampton, When was that?	Um, when I was four.	

		Giles Cooper	Sandra Smith
Q.12	Who is the man who sees you when you are ill?	The doctor.	The doctor.
Q.13.	Why are people sometimes ill?	Well they catch it, sometimes.	Because they don't feel well.
P.	Why don't they feel well?		Sometimes people have an headache and a got colds.
P.	Why do people sometimes have a headache and got colds?		Because they catch it.
P.	They catch what?	. . . the illness, you know chicken-pox and all sorts of things.	
P.	So why are they ill?	Well they catch it from other people or sometimes they just get it through eating too much.	
P.	Why does that make them ill?	Um. I don't know.	
Q.14.	Why shouldn't you hit children smaller than yourself?	Because they're younger than you, and they, that ma' takes . . . hurts, be naughty, and get told off by themself.	'Cos that is naughty.
P.	Why shouldn't you hit children younger than you?	Because you think it might not hurt but it does, to them . . .	
P.	And why shouldn't you hurt them?	Because it's naughty, to do it.	
P.	Why is it naughty?	Well you shouldn't do anything like it. You should	

		Giles Cooper	*Sandra Smith*
		only play with your own size of children, and do it to them.	
P.	Why is it naughty?		'Cos if you hit them the little girl she'll go and tell mum.
P.	Why will she go and tell mum?		'Cos someone hit her.
Q.15.	Can you tell me how to ride a bicycle?	You pedal it by the pedals at the bottom.	Pedal the wheels.
Q.16.	Why does wood float?	Well, wood can float because when it goes on the water it is light and when it goes on it won't sink because the water's calm.	'Cos it's light.
P.	So why does, why do light things float?	Um, 'cos the water you know, carries them along by	
P.	Why does the water carry them along?	'Cos the water's moving along.	
P.	Why does it float because it's light?		'Cos it's a bit of wood.
P.	Because it's a bit of wood. So why does it float?		'Cos it's light.
Q.17.	Where does milk come from?	Cows.	Cows.
P.	And why do cows give milk?	Well, they're the best animals that make the stuff that we drink.	
P.	But why do they make it?	Because they eat the grass that's got the stuff that they er makes into milk.	

M

		Giles Cooper	Sandra Smith
P.	And why does that happen? Why do they eat grass and make it into milk?	Well, they have to eat the grass because um or we wouldn't have any milk at all.	
P.	Why do cows give milk?		Because it's cream.
Q.18.	When was your birthday?	Um in May.	June.
Q.19.	What are birthdays for?	. . . it's, birthdays are for because when it's the day when you were born and you were christened in church.	How old you get.
Q.20.	Why shouldn't anyone tell lies?	Because it's naughty and they don't want, they shouldn't tell them.	'Cos it's naughty.
P.	Why shouldn't they tell them?	Well, they'll believe you and go and do it instead and then they, they will get them into trouble if they've been naughty and . . . say they didn't do it.	
P.	And why mustn't you get them into trouble?	Because, because you shouldn't get them into trouble because it's naughty to get them into trouble. You should own up to the person and tell them they, you did it.	

		Giles Cooper	Sandra Smith
P.	Why is it naughty?		Because you get told off if you tell lies.
P.	Why do you get told off if you tell lies?		You get told off for telling lies, but you should tell the truth.
Q.21.	Why does Daddy shave every morning?	'Cos he doesn't want to grow a beard.	He shaves because he's got to go to work.
P.	Why doesn't he want to grow a beard?	Well, some people don't like growing beards, and some people do.	
P.	These people who don't like wearing beards, why don't they like wearing beards?	Well, they think they'll look ugly	
P.	Why does he shave because he's got to go to work?		'Cos he's got important business.
P.	Why has he got important business?		He's got important business with the firm.
Q.22.	How tall would you like to be when you are grown up?	About six feet.	As tall as you grow.
Q.23.	Why do the leaves fall off the trees?	Because the tree waits for sucks up the water and saves it for winter and when they do the leaves want water and they drop off, and die, and they die and fall off the tree.	When it's autumn.
P.	Why do they die?	Because they are not having water.	
P.	And why aren't they	Because the tree	

		Giles Cooper	Sandra Smith
	getting water?	isn't sucking it up to the leaves.	
P.	Why isn't the tree sucking it up?	Well, it's sucking the water from the ground to save it for winter.	
P.	Why do the leaves fall off the tree when it's autumn?		'Cos the wind blows them off.
P.	Why do the leaves fall off the trees in autumn because the wind blows them off?		Don't know.
Q.24.	How do the leaves fall off the trees?	Well um, they break off the branch. The branch gets too old and falls and um then sometimes that happens to the leaves, they get too old and break off their stem and fall.	When it's windy.
Q.25.	Why does a ball come down when you throw it up in the air?	Well, um when you throw it it can go only a so' a distance and then it'll fall down. Air is stop stop blowing it down you know, it just falls down because the wind stops blowing.	'Cos the wind blows it down again.
P.	Why does it fall down because the wind stops blowing?	Because the wind's not blowing any more.	
P.	When the wind stops, why does it fall?	Um, 'cos the wind's not blowing it any more and um	

	Giles Cooper	Sandra Smith
	all that it does is just let it drop.	
P. Why does the wind blow it down again?		'Cos the wind the wind blows it down and the girl catches it.
P. Why does the wind blow it down and the girl catches it?		Don't know.
Q.26. Why shouldn't anyone steal?	Because um they should steal because they're naughty to steal the things and they only get into trouble with the police.	'Cos that's robbery.
P. Why will they get into trouble with the police?	Because they've been stealing from other people's house.	
P. But when you're stealing from other people, why do the police come after you?	Because they want to find out why you did it and do it and tell of you.	
P. So can you tell me why shouldn't you do it?	Because it's naughty and just the police will be after you and you can go to court and you can go to jail.	
P. Why is that robbery?		Robbery, robbery is stealing.
P. Why shouldn't anyone steal?		'Cos it's naughty.
P. Why is it naughty?		'Cos if they steal things the police will get them.
Q.27. Why does the sea have waves?	Well it has waves because the wind	To help the wa', to help the water go.

		Giles Cooper	*Sandra Smith*
		blows it along and the ships make the waves when they go past.	
P.	Why does the wind make the waves?	Because it's blowing on the sea and the sea goes up and then goes down and it carries on when the wind still blow.	
P.	Why does that happen?	Er, because um, when the a' it blows the sea um, it'll keep on blowing it until it gets to the end of the sea and it will stop blowing and go and blow another one while, when the other ones at the end another one will still be on its way.	
P.	Why to help the water go?		'Cos if the water goes slow it don't go too fast.
Q.28.	Where does the water in the tap come from?	Um the sea.	From the sea.
Q.29.	Why should children do what their parents tell them to?	Well, if they don't they'll be in trouble and you might get a smack or um they might er be told off and um make them do it again and have to do it.	Because they got to.
P.	Why will they get a smack if they don't do	Well, they shouldn't um	

	Giles Cooper	Sandra Smith
what they are told to?	smack, they shouldn't do, they should do what their mother says and then when they do tell them what they should do um you er you should do it or you know you'll get into trouble.	
P. But why should you do it?	'Cos your parents would like you to do it.	
P. Why have they got to?		'Cos if the children don't do what their parents say their mothers will tell them off.
P. Why will their mothers tell them off?		'Cos the mo' if their mother tells them to do something they got to do it.
Q.30. Tell me all the different things you can do with a piece of string.	Make lassos, tie people up, um you can um make you can use string for pulling sails up a ship and um you can make bows and arrows, you make a bow, and you can play a game you can tie them on to an apple and try to eat it without using your hands.	You can skip with it. You can jump over it. You can play skipping with your mates with it. You can play jumping over it.

References

AREWA, E. O., and DUNDES, A., 'Proverbs and the Ethnography of Speaking Folklore', Gumperz, J. J., and Hymes, D. (eds), Spec. Ed., *Amer. Anthrop.*, (1964), lxvi, 70–85.

ATKINSON, J. W. (ed.), *Motives in Fantasy, Action and Society*, New York: Van Nostrand, 1957.

BECKER, W. C., 'Consequences of Different Kinds of Parental Discipline', in Hoffman, M. L., and Hoffman, L. W. (eds.), *Child Development Research*, i, New York: Russell Sage, 1964.

BERLYNE, D. E., *Conflict, Arousal and Curiosity*, New York: McGraw-Hill, 1960.

BERNSTEIN, B. B., 'Some Sociological Determinants of Perception', *Brit. J. Sociol.* (1958), ix, 159–74.

'Social Structure, Language and Learning', *Educ. Res.* (1961a), iii, 163–76.

'Social Class and Linguistic Development'; in Halsay, A. H., Floud, J. and Anderson, A. (eds), *Education, Economy and Society*, Free Press, 1961(b).

'Linguistic Codes, Hesitation Phenomena and Intelligence', *Language and Speech*, (1962a), v, 31–46.

'Social Class, Linguistic Codes and Grammatical Elements', *Language and Speech*, (1962b), v, 221–40.

and YOUNG, D., 'Social Class Differences in Conceptions of the Use of Toys', *Sociology* (1967), i, 131–40.

BRAITHWAITE, R. B., *Scientific Explanation*, Cambridge Univ. Press, 1954.

BRANDIS, W., and HENDERSON, D., *Social Class, Language and Communication*, London: Routledge, 1970.

BRONFENBRENNER, U., 'Socialization and Social Class through Time and Space', in Maccoby, E. E., Newcombe, T. M., and Hartley, E. L. (eds), *Readings in Social Psychology*, New York: Holt, 1958, 400–25.

CAZDEN, C. B., 'Subcultural Differences in Child Language', *Merrill-Palmer Qtly.* (1966), xii, 185–219.

CENTRAL ADVISORY COUNCIL FOR EDUCATION (ENGLAND), *Early Leaving*, London: H.M.S.O., 1954.

15 to 18 (Crowther), London: H.M.S.O., 1959.

Half Our Future (Newsom), London: H.M.S.O., 1963 (a).

Children and Their Primary Schools (Plowden), London: H.M.S.O., 1966.

CHOMSKY, N., *Syntactic Structures*, The Hague: Mouton, 1957.

Aspects of the Theory of Syntax, Cambridge, Mass.: M.I.T. Press, 1965.

CLAUSEN, J. A., 'Family Structure, Socialization and Personality', in Hoffman, M. L., and Hoffman, L. W. (eds), *Child Development Research*, ii, New York: Russell Sage, 1964.

COMMITTEE ON HIGHER EDUCATION, *Higher Education (Robbins)*, London: H.M.S.O., 1963 (b).

COOK, J., 'An Inquiry into Patterns of Communication and Control between Mothers and Children in Different Social Classes', Ph.D. thesis, Univ. of London, 1971.

COULTHARD, R. M., and ROBINSON, W. P., 'The Structure of the Nominal Group and Elaboratedness of Code', *Language and Speech* (1968), *xi*, 234–50.

DEUTSCH, M., *The Disadvantaged Child*, New York: Basic Books, 1967.

DIXON, R. M. W., *Linguistic Science and Logic*, The Hague: Mouton, 1963.

DOUGLAS, J. W. B., *The Home and the School*, London: MacGibbon & Kee, 1964.

DURKHEIM, E., *The Division of Labour in Society* (1st ed., 1893), trans. G. Simpson, New York: Free Press, 1949.

ELLIS, J., 'On Contextual Meaning', in Bazell, C. E., Catford, J. C., Halliday, M.A.K., and Robins, R. H. (eds), *In Memory of J. R. Firth*, London: Longmans, 1966.

ERVIN TRIPP, S. M., 'An Analysis of the Interaction of Language, Topic, and Listener', in *The Ethnology of Communication*, Gumperz, J. J., and Hymes, D. (eds), *Amer. Anthropologist* (1964), lxvi, 86–102.

'Sociolinguistics' in Berkowitz, L. (ed.), *Advances in Experimental Social Psychology* (1969), iii, New York: Academic Press.

FOWLER, H., *Curiosity and Exploratory Behaviour,* New York: Macmillan, 1963.

FLAVELL, J. H., *The Development of Role-taking and Communication Skills in Children*, New York: Wiley, 1968.

GAHAGAN, D. and G., *Talk Reform: an Exploratory Language Programme for Infant School Children*, London: Routledge, 1970.

GOLDMAN-EISLER, F., 'Hesitation and Information in Speech', in Cherry, C. (ed.), *Information Theory*, 4th London Symposium, Butterworth, 1961.

HALLIDAY, M. A. K., MCINTOSH, A., and STEVENS, P., *The Linguistic Sciences and Language Teaching*, London: Longmans, 1964.

HAWKINS, P., 'Social Class, the Nominal Group and Reference', *Language and Speech* (1969), *xii*, 125–35.

HESS, R. D., and SHIPMAN, V. C., 'Cognitive Elements in Maternal Behaviour', in Hill, J. P. (ed.), *Minnesota Symposia on Child Psychology*, i, Minneapolis: Univ. of Minnesota, 1967.

HYMES, D., 'Models of the Interaction of Language and Social Setting', *J. Soc. Iss.* (1967), xxiii, 8–28.

IRWIN, D. C., 'Infant Speech: the Effect of Family Occupational Status and of Age on Use of Sound Types', *J. Speech Hearing Disorders* (1948), xiii, 223–6.

ISAACS, N., *Appendix on Children's 'Why' Questions*, London, 1930.

JONES, D., *An Outline of English Phonetics* (8th ed.), Cambridge: Heffer, 1956.

JONES, J., 'Social Class and the Under-fives', *New Society* (1966), *ccxxi*, 935–6.

JOOS, M., 'The Five Clocks', *Internat. J. Amer. Linguistics*, xxviii, Part 5, 1962.

KATZ, J. J., and FODOR, J. A., 'The Structure of a Semantic Theory', *Language* (1963), xxxix, 170–210.

KOHLBERG, L., 'Stage and Sequence in Moral Development', in Goslin, D. (ed.), *Handbook of Socialization Theory and Research*, Chicago: Rand McNally, 1969.

KOHN, M. L., 'Social Class and Parent-child Relationships: an Interpretation', *Amer. J. Sociol.* (1963), lxviii, 471–80.

LABOV, W., *The Social Stratification of English in New York City*, Washington, D.C.,: Center for Applied Linguistics, 1966.

LAWTON, D., 'Social Class Differences in Language Development', *Language and Speech* (1963), vi, 120–43.

'Social Class Language Differences in Group Discussions', *Language and Speech* (1964), vii, 182–204.

Social Class, Language and Education, London: Routledge, 1968.

LOVELL, K., *An Introduction to Human Development*, London: Macmillan, 1968.

MEDAWAR, P. B., *The Art of the Soluble*, London: Methuen, 1967.

MORTON-WILLIAMS, ROMA, and FINCH, S., Schools Council Enquiry, 1, *Young School Leavers*, London: H.M.S.O., 1968.

PEI, M., *Glossary of Linguistic Terminology*, Columbia Univ. Press, 1966.

PIAGET, J., *The Language and Thought of the Child*, London: Routledge, 1926.
The Child's Conception of Physical Causality, London: Routledge, 1930.
The Moral Judgement of the Child, London: Routledge, 1932.
The Psychology of Intelligence, London: Routledge, 1950.

RACKSTRAW, S. J., and ROBINSON, W. P., 'Social and Psychological Factors associated with Variability of Answering Behaviour in Five-year-old Children', *Language and Speech* (1967), x, 88–106.

RAVEN, J. C., *The Crichton Vocabulary Scale*, London: Lewis, 1951.

ROBINSON, W. P., 'Close Procedure for the Investigation of Social-class Differences in Language Usage', *Language and Speech* (1962a), viii, 45–55.
'The Elaborated Code in Working-class Language', *Language and Speech* (1962b), viii, 243–52.
'Restricted Codes in Sociolinguistics and the Sociology of Education', in Whiteley, W. B. (ed.), *Language and Social Change*, Oxford Univ. Press, 1970(a).
Language as a Socio-cultural Determinant of Learning, Hamburg: UNESCO Institute for Education, 1970(b).
and CREED, C. D., 'Perceptual and Verbal Discriminations of "Elaborated" and "Restricted" Code Users', *Language and Speech* (1968), xi, 182–93.
and RACKSTRAW, S. J., 'Variations in Mothers' Answers to Children's Questions as a Function of Social Class, Verbal Intelligence Test Scores and Sex', *Sociology* (1967), i, 259–76.

SCHATZMAN, R., and STRAUSS, A., 'Social Class and Modes of Communication', *Amer. J. Sociol.* (1955), lx, 329–38.

SINCLAIR, J. MCH., 'Beginning the Study of Lexis', in Bazell, C. E., Catford, J. C., Halliday, M. A. K., and Robins, R. H. (eds), *In Memory of J. R. Firth*, London: Longmans, 1966.

SKINNER, B. F., *Verbal Behaviour*, New York: Appleton-Century-Crofts, 1957.

TEMPLIN, M. C., *Certain Language Skills in Children: Their Development and Interrelationships*, Minneapolis: Univ. Minnesota Press, 1957.

TURNER, G. J., and MOHAN, B. A., *A Linguistic Description and Computer Program for Children's Speech*, London: Routledge, 1970.

URE, J. N., and RODGER, A., ' "*Cargoes*", a Linguistic Study of a Literary Text', undated, unpublished, ms.

VERNON, P. E., *Intelligence and Cultural Environment*, London: Methuen, 1969.

VYGOTSKY, L. S., *Thought and Language*, New York: Wiley, 1962.

WECHSLER, D., *Wechsler Intelligence Scale for Children: Manual*, New York: Psychol. Corp., 1949.

WISEMAN, S., *Education and Environment*, Manchester Univ. Press, 1964.

ZIPF, G. K., *The Psycho-biology of Language*, New York: Houghton Mifflin, 1935.

Author Index

Note: Page numbers printed in italics refer to Volume II

Allport, G. W., 114
Arewa, C. O., 73
Atkinson, J. W., 8
Becker, W. C., 10
Berlyne, D. E., 8
Bernstein, B., 2, 11, 12, 35, 70–1, 72, 73, 75, 93–5, 96, 97, 98, 103, 112, 113, 115, 116, 117, 119, 121, 127, 146, 148, 150, 152–7 *passim*, *183*, *292*
Braithwaite, R. B., 66
Brandis, W., 6, 96, 99, 113, 126, 127, 150, 156
Brimer, M. A., 78, 126
Bronfenbrenner, U., 10
Cazden, C., 10
Central Advisory Council for Education, 11
Chomsky, N., 71, *vii*, *182*
Clausen, J. A., 10
Cook, J., 116–17, 127, 154, 156
Coulthard, C. M., 126
Creed, C. D., 115, 126
Deutsch, M., 10
Dixon, R. M. W., 39
Douglas, J. W. B., 11
Dundas, A., 73
Dunn, L. M., 78, 126
Ellis, J., 26, 28
Ervin-Tripp, S., 10–11, 29
Finch, S., 11
Flavell, J. H., 35
Fodor, J. A., 21
Fowler, H., 8
Gahagan, D. H. and G., 7, 121, 126
Goldman-Eisler, F., 114
Halliday, M. A. K., 28, 30, 38, 80, 97
Hawkins, P., 115, 152
Henderson, D., 6, 96, 99, 113, 126, 127, 150, 156

Hess, R. B., 154, 156
Hymes, D., 10
Irwin, O. C., 10
Isaacs, N., 123
Jones, D., 19, 96, 156
Joos, M., 29
Katz, J. J., 21
Kohlberg, L., 9, 148, 154, *251*
Labov, W. A., 29
Lawton, D., 115
Lovell, K., 148
McIntosh, A., 28, 38, 97
Medawar, P. S., 121
Mohan, B. A., 50n., 80
Morton-Williams, R., 11
Pei, M., 38
Piaget, J., 9, 93–4, 117, 123, 148, *251*
Rackstraw, S. J., 75n., *257*
Raven, J. C., 78
Robinson, W. P., 11, 75n., 115, 126, *257*, *291*
Schatzman, R., 35
Shipman, V. C., 10, 154, 156
Sinclair, A., 39
Skinner, B. F., 71
Strauss, A., 35
Strevens, P., 28, 38, 97
Templin, M. C., 10
Turner, G. J., 50n., 80
Ure, J. N., 28
Vernon, P. E., 11
Vygotsky, L. S., 94
Wechsler, D., 123
Wiseman, S., 11
Young, D., 113, 150, 156
Zipf, G. K., 68

Subject Index

Note: Page numbers printed in italics refer to Volume II

accuracy of mothers' answers, 97, 98, 100, 101, 106, 112, 113, 153, 156–7; *see also* truth
adjuncts, 152; in mothers' answers (simplifying), 103, 108, 109, 114, (uninformative), 102, 108, 109, 114
analogy (appeals to), 65, 74, 98, 110,

118, 122, 134, 147, 153, *245*, *290*, *314*, *331*
answers: criteria for separating from non-answers, 23–4; definition, 22–3; description, 25–48; form, 23 (*see* grammar; lexis); length, 276–7; *see also* context; mode, etc.